MW01064395

THE MAGNIFICENT CHURCH

HAVING A HEALTHY CHURCH IN AN UNHEALTHY AGE

—ᛥ—

by

Bill Campbell

PRESS

DEDICATION

—∿—

The author wishes to dedicate this volume with love to his wife Sue, who now understands the painful experiences involved in giving birth to a book.

Table of Contents

—w—

Preface

—ɯ—

This is the author's second book. Following the completion of the first volume, someone said that after writing one book no one should ever do such a foolish thing again. Experiencing the difficulties associated with writing a book did cause a chuckle. Yet, the first attempt did not cause the pen to be laid down, or, to let up on the computer keys. Rather, there was a desire to begin the next volume.

Deepest appreciation is expressed to those who offered encouragements and compliments on the first book. The results were most gratifying.

In the first volume attention was focused on, *The Magnificent Journey*. An attempt was made to assist the reader in viewing the Christian life through the lens of heaven. The Christian life is a much more winsome and exciting venture when a believer has his or her focus set on heaven.

In the second volume a transition is made from the Christian life to the church. While the author deeply loves the church, there is a need to acknowledge its shortcomings. Congregations are not perfect. They never have been. They never will be. Thus, while commending the church, its problem areas will also be highlighted. The reader will be offered some light for solving the ills of the church, as the author does not wish to be a destructive critic. Insights for making the church better for our children and grandchildren are needed to bequeath to them a healthy church.

The goal is not to shape the church as the author wants to shape it. Rather, there is a vision for the church to meet the needs of coming generations. The aim is to have a magnificent church for those who will assume the future bridal of leadership.

Magnificent continues to be used in the book title. The idea for using this word was not the author's. Instead, the author's son, Matt, recommended the continuation of the word in future volumes.

Thus, with Matt's suggestion, the title will shift from, *The Magnificent Journey*, to *The Magnificent Church*. The concern in the second volume is with having a healthy church in an age where congregational ill health is the growing problem.

Perhaps there is a need to explain the meaning of the word magnificent. When labeling the church as magnificent, it is not meant to suggest the church is perfect. Rather, magnificent is used following the lead of Webster, who defines a magnificent church as one representing the outstanding of its kind. In short, it serves as a living model to follow by other churches. If this volume helps in bringing congregational magnificence to fruition, then the author's efforts will have been amply rewarded.

Introduction

—ɯ—

S ome congregations can be described as healthy. Other congregations are better described as unhealthy. What factors will help to determine whether your congregation is a healthy or an unhealthy fellowship? This question may appear simple to answer at first. Yet, it becomes difficult to resolve once it is pondered at length.

The traditional way individuals have identified a congregation's state of health is in regard to its progress. In other words, is the congregation growing? If a congregation is not growing then disease is considered as the right diagnosis. If this is the correct analysis, then there are more unhealthy congregations in existence today than healthy ones.

Being aware of numerous ill congregations, the spiritual leader needs to position himself or herself as a health diagnostician. The health diagnostician is concerned with uncovering congregational disease. Not only does he seek to detect disease, he will endeavor to assist a congregation in alleviating its illness. He will keep his finger on a congregation's pulse. Serious dangers lie ahead for a congregation without this important assistance.

The major reason for congregational illness today is thought by many to be related to its present dismal state of health. While this is the current problem, it has not always been so. There was a time when churches were healthy. Persons were being drawn to them. Church attendance was increasing. Lives were being changed. A number of these congregations are now declining, however, and they face the possibility of nonexistence. Like the dinosaurs of old, they are confronted with the danger of extinction.[1]

Rick Warren arrested the author's attention regarding congregational ill health when he stated: "I believe the key issue for churches in the twenty-first century will be church health, not church growth."[2] Before reading Warren, the author was in agreement with his point of view. The ultimate aim of the church is to grow, but the growth of the church is heavily dependent on its state of health.

Like the song of old, "love and marriage, love and marriage, they go together like a horse and carriage." So do church health and church growth. Congregations will grow if they are healthy. Conversely, congregations will not grow if they are unhealthy.

Churches are unhealthy today, in large part, because Christian discipleship is often absent. Persons were once converted and discipled. Over time, however, being a Christian was connected with an institutional form of religious commitment. And Christians, along with their churches, lost touch with the need for discipleship development and training.

Christian discipleship was exchanged for church membership. And church members have chosen to settle into an institutional posture. To reverse this sad condition will be a Herculean challenge for the greatest of spiritual gladiators.

The call of Jesus needs to be read again carefully by those who have chosen to follow Him: "If anyone desires to come after Me, let him deny himself, and take up his cross, and follow Me" (Matthew 16:24). Persons were not summoned by Jesus to be members of a church. They were called to be His followers. Yet, many have become churchmen, in place of being disciplined Christian disciples. This is a serious problem congregations need to courageously address.

Paul Nixon has given a helpful analogy for better understanding an ailing church. He identifies congregational illness
with the term, amnesia.[3] Amnesia is a state in which one
forgets his or her past life. Ones personal history is erased,
much like words are removed from a slate or blackboard.
Some victims are able to recover from amnesia. Many others,
however, are unable to conquer the forgetfulness continuing
to hover over them.

What is true of individuals is also true of churches. Many
congregations are in the throes of spiritual amnesia. They
have forgotten who or what they are. Their true identity has
become a mystery. Their actions are largely unexplainable.
They are functioning with an unclear sense of direction.
If they cannot be snapped out of their stupor, they will be
faced with spending the remainder of their days in a round
of meaningless church activities.

Spiritual amnesia has also brought another evil in its train.
Specifically, the church has become like society in place of
becoming the salt and light Jesus intended (see Matthew
5:13-16). God has designed the church to be His presence
in society. Yet, society has gotten the upper hand. Society is
influencing the church more than the church is influencing
society. It is similar to a few bad apples in a barrel of good

apples. Unless the bad apples are removed, their evil influence will, like a cancer, destroy the other good apples.

The purpose in this volume is to awaken the church out of its amnesia, in short, to see the church overcome its forgetfulness. A healthy church is the needed catalyst to effectively change a fragmented community and world.

A course of action is being prescribed in this book that will serve to reclaim our congregations. If the map offered is followed faithfully, it will bring a congregation back to renewed life. Furthermore, it will enable a congregation to make positive steps in the direction of being a magnificent church.

Without this intentional movement toward magnificence the church will continue in its crippled condition, and remain oblivious to its mission. The church's mission is to make Christian disciples. Apart from disciple making, a church has lost its way. When a church loses its way it becomes but another institution unable to make a lasting difference in persons lives in these times.

Church's mission is to make Christian disciples.

SETTING THE STAGE

—∿—

*"I beg each of you to develop a passionate and
public hatred of bureaucracy."*
(Tom Peters)

*"If you want to make enemies,
try to change something."*
(Woodrow Wilson)

Chapter One

Two Examples

Consider two Midwestern congregations. One is a
mainline denominational church. The other is an
independent church. Both congregations are located in a
mid-sized American city. The area in which both congregations exist is flourishing, and is an excellent location for a
church to grow. Both congregations began at approximately
the same time forty years ago.

Yet, there is an important difference between the two churches. The mainline congregation is experiencing phenomenal growth. Their Sunday morning worship attendance is four thousand. On the other hand, the conservative independent congregation is dying. A recent report revealed the foregoing congregation was below fifty in Sunday morning worship attendance.

At one time, the conservative independent congregation was having three hundred and fifty in its attendance. Over time, however, it began to slowly decline.

The mainline congregation has done the opposite. Rather than decline they have continued to grow. Many persons have been added to their church. The remarkable growth of this congregation has forced the church to relocate to another site allowing them more room to grow.

Should you drive by the property of either congregation you would notice some obvious differences. The conservative independent congregation appears to be a ghost town. This conclusion comes from two observations. For one thing, very little activity is going on around their building. And secondly, the building facility reveals signs of deterioration, and is in need of repair.

A different picture is noted, however, if you drive by the facility of the mainline church. A beautiful structure grabs your attention. Along with the attractive facility is considerable activity. People are entering and leaving their building. Should you look more closely at this congregation you will also discover serious engagement in ministry. Specifically, there are a number of need meeting ministries in place. The mainline church is also reaching out to people around them and seeking to meet their spiritual needs. *Are we doing this - if so how?*

On the other hand, the conservative independent congregation opens its doors and anticipates persons will come and join them. Yet, this is not happening. The independent church is continuing to die. But the mainline church is continuing to experience significant growth.

Now some questions. Why is the mainline congregation growing? Why is the conservative independent congregation dying? Church leaders everywhere are asking these questions. They want to know how a non-growing church can become a growing church. Even a casual diagnosis will lead to the conclusion one of the congregations is healthy, whereas the other congregation is unhealthy. This is the correct assessment as God has designed His church to grow.

Yet, if a church is not growing then something is wrong health wise.

The problem discussed here also applies to businesses. One business is growing. A business next door to it is not growing. Churches can learn from successful and growing businesses.[4] Businesses can also learn some important lessons from growing and successful congregations.

There is another item to be noted about the two congregations being profiled. Growing congregations are positive and forward looking. Dying congregations are negative and looking backward. They also engage incessantly in complaining and idle talk. Growing congregations are also busy, but their activity is not with idle talk and complaining. Rather, they are focused on ministry and how they can be more effective in serving and meeting the needs of persons around them.

We are now in a position to take a reflective look at what makes a congregation healthy. All the author has shared up to this point is intended to prepare for this moment of clarity and insight.

Yet, some leading questions need to be posed. First of all, what are the major ingredients for a healthy congregation? Conversely, what ingredients contribute toward a congregation being afflicted with ill health? Stated another way, what enables a congregation to be magnificent in place of being a congregation suffering from malignancy?

Consider the differences between these two churches. The approach will be to contrast them through the use of a visual table. As the comparison is made, we are in a better position to understand what makes a congregation either a healthy, or, an unhealthy church body.

Why Churches Are Healthy	Why Churches Are Unhealthy
They possess vision	They lack vision
They have long term pastoral ministry tenure	They have short term pastoral ministry tenure
They free their pastoral ministers to provide leadership	They restrict pastoral ministry leadership- pastoral ministers are viewed as "hired hands"
They focus on others	They focus on themselves
They focus on positive issues	They focus on negative issues
They provide leadership	They practice management and control
They have concern for the present and the future	They have concern for their past history and seek to relive it in the present

They function as a spiritual organism	They function as a business/organization
They involve others	They limit the involvement of others
They attract a wide variety of people	They attract their own kind
They are open to new and creative methods	They are closed to new and creative methods
They concern themselves with developing relationships	They concern themselves with enforcing rules and regulations
They are focused on ministry and outreach	They are focused on organizational maintenance
They have mixed ages among them	They have only advanced ages among them

Allow the author to share a final sad feature occurring in non-growing congregations. They enjoy making critical remarks about successful churches. Non-growing congregations seek to justify their failure to grow through negative comments like the following ones:

- "At least we're a congregation that stands for the truth, and are firm in what we believe, unlike some congregations we know!"

- "I'm not comfortable with a large church! In fact, a large church gives me a cold feeling! No church should be too large!"
- "Large churches are guilty of giving people what they want in place of giving them what they need!"

In this book the author wants to offer his continuing diagnosis of what makes a church unhealthy. He nonetheless wants to offer some major benchmarks for congregations that cause them to stand out as model churches of health. In short, he wants to give a snapshot of a magnificent church. A church, in other words, that is a healthy church for these unhealthy times in which we live.

The author is anxious to continue this important journey. Join him as he makes the pilgrimage toward healthy church life.

Congregational Leadership

What factors enable a congregation to be a magnificent church, as opposed to being a malignant church? What makes a church healthy, in other words, in place of being an unhealthy church? Is there a clear path to follow in order to arrive at the entry way to magnificence?

Should a formula be instantly obtainable, a long line of congregations would form to secure the magic potion. This would occur because a large number of congregations are at a loss today to know how to reverse their downward slide.

The author wishes he had the ability to produce the instant formula required for healing an ailing congregation. It would definitely help ease much of the anxiety and concern surrounding church life today. Furthermore, it would help ease the role of church leaders and make their efforts much less stressful. But no one has been able to identify this quick-fix potion to instantly heal unhealthy churches.

One major reason has been discovered, however, for much of the present congregational dysfunction being experienced. The most lethal area of congregational malignancy is connected with having the wrong kind of leadership. If the leadership issue is not seriously addressed today, congregations will continue to be destroyed.

Allow this matter to be stated even more clearly. In far too many congregations they are greatly under-led. Furthermore, leadership is being replaced by iron-fisted management. Management is necessary. Yet, extreme management without leadership will bring a congregation to ashes. For iron-fisted controllers bring abnormal fear into congregational settings.

A brief picture needs to be given of how a controller operates. Controllers rise to the top of organizations much like cream rises to the top of a jar of milk. They will generally be the outspoken members of a group. If not outspoken, they will work undercover to influence persons to help them achieve their agenda.

Sometimes controllers will appoint themselves as CEO'S in an organization. At other times, persons in the organization will appoint them as their ultimate voice of authority.

Seldom do controllers acquire instant charge of any organization. Their control will develop slowly. Once their cleats are dug in, however, removing them from power will be a task beyond the abilities and powers of a mighty gladiator to achieve.

Controllers are frightening. It is best to remain as far away from a controller as one can get. They are very cold and calculating. They are rigid and regimented. They are demanding and devilish. The sound of their voice, the look in their eyes, and their general body language, all serve to remind one that they are power driven, and wish to be in control.

It is also important to remind the reader of another fact. The controller knows he or she is in charge. In fact, in a short time one will discover they own the floor. Seldom will a controller treat anyone warmly, unless they are preparing the person to side with them in an important matter involving their personal agenda. A controller has as many colors as a chameleon. And their colors will change with the dictates of the agenda they have established.

Additionally, controllers expect the people around them to play by the rules. And controllers know the rules. They know them very well. Controllers are better at understanding the rules than attorneys are at interpreting the law.

But one will soon learn the rules being followed are the rules of the controller. Furthermore, a person is expected to play by their established rules. A rule that is not the controllers rule cannot be included in the overall game plan.

Controllers not only frighten the author, they frighten him as well with what they can do to an organization. Their approach is paralyzing. They will freeze an organization much like a freezer will freeze water in an ice tray.

A controller's special ability is to establish his or her reign of fear. As they function, they will expect to be the one who rubber stamps any idea or action introduced. If you do not have the controller's approval, you will be unable to make headway with any effort or plan.

Those who choose not to agree with a controller are eventually driven out of an organization. Many have discovered the cunning ability of a controller by being removed from an organization by one of them. There is no other way to go but the controller's way.

Controllers have been considered in terms of organizations generally. And they are in every conceivable organization today. Yet, they are also in churches. They have invaded the sacred precincts. That is not supposed to happen. Yet, it is happening in growing numbers of congregations. Controllers have representatives among a congregations leadership. They will nonetheless rise up within the general membership of a congregation to push their agendas in subtle and political ways.

Visionary Leadership

Controllers are clearly a formidable problem for all organizations. But they are a very formidable problem for congregations today. Thus, a need exists to make an important shift in thinking. Specifically, a church leadership model is needed to replace the current controlling model imprisoning and destroying congregations.

The model needed today is visionary leadership. Congregations are healthy when visionary leadership is in place. Congregations are unhealthy when controlling leaders enslave a congregation to their agenda. This controlling leadership style causes the suffering, dysfunction, and unrest that is present in many congregations.

Yet, the visionary leadership called for here needs further clarification. This is required because a considerable difference exists between management when compared with leadership. Management is not leadership, nor is leadership management. Both functions are necessary, yet they each fulfill a distinct and separate role.

Warren Bennis and Burt Nanus state the issue correctly when they give these functions the following definition: "managers do things right, leaders do the right things."[5] Bennis and Nanus' definition means managers are focused on giving direction to things already existing. Leaders, on the other hand, see what is missing in their organization and seek to put it in place. In fact, a true leader will not only recognize what is needed, they will possess a burning passion to see their vision take shape and become reality.

Their heart is on fire with the vision. The great obstacle a leader faces is being able to bring others in the organization on board to share his or her vision.

It is not the author's intention here to establish the need for leadership and then discard management. For both functions need to be in place. Each of the functions complement the other. Yet, in many instances congregations are over-managed and they are under-led. There is an overabundance of congregational managers with a serious corresponding dearth of visionary leaders who are free to function and give visionary direction to a congregation. In some instances this problem exists because of a misunderstanding in the leadership role. At other times, it exists because congregational controllers emerge and take a congregation hostage.

The losses emerging from the absence of visionary leadership should be the matter of greatest concern:

- The loss of visionary leadership has served, for one thing, to suffocate many churches. Critical decision making and action have been by-passed. Furthermore, congregations have become paralyzed and are monuments of past achievements. They are sitting and not serving. Ill health abounds in them, and the laments

Stop Churches need to be serving

regarding these congregations can be heard from both near and far.

- The loss of visionary leadership has also placed churches in a non-growth mode. The church was designed by God to grow. But excessive management has stifled congregations, making it impossible for them to experience growth. They must be led, and not just managed, if they are going to experience the advancement and progress needed today.

- The loss of visionary leadership in congregations has nonetheless caused some of the finest young men and women to resent established churches. Even if they attend these congregations they will predictably choose to be uninvolved in them, which is due in large part to the presence of iron-fisted congregational controllers.

- The loss of visionary leadership has also caused persons in communities to stay away from established churches. They want to be part of something making a major community difference. They do not wish to identify with a religious organization perpetuating maintenance, or, "keeping things as they are."

Visionary leadership is clearly a crucial quality for having a healthy congregation in the present time. But what steps need to be taken to pave the way for visionary leadership in churches? Consider the following steps:

- Congregations need to be sure when conversions take place these conversions are to Christ, and not just simply to the church. The foregoing error has spawned institutional thinking today, and institutional thinking has replaced kingdom thinking.

- Congregations exist to make disciples. The church is not in existence to elevate itself, or, its own image. Every decision made by congregational leaders should be directed toward the process of making disciples.

- Congregations need leaders who are Christians and not simply churchmen. Many congregations place persons in leadership roles through group popularity, or, for political reasons. Sometimes they are even placed in leadership because there is no one else available to serve. Yet, if a leader is not a Christian leader a congregation is headed for unhealthy times ahead.

- Congregations need those serving as leaders who are there for the right reason. Donald H. McGannon states the matter best here: "Leadership is action, not position." Anyone who wishes to serve as a church leader, because of a desire for recognition and position, is there for the wrong reason.

The author has endeavored to set the stage in the opening chapter for what will follow in the remainder of the book. It is the conviction of the author the major problems being experienced in church life today are connected with those individuals who have been allowed to practice iron-fisted control in congregations.

Author's conviction

What practical handles are available for helping see how iron-fisted persons go about exercising control? The chapter which follows will introduce the reader to a visual framework for seeing a congregational controller in action. The reader is invited to take a careful look at the various angles from which to get a glimpse of a congregational controller.

Reflections

1. Does size indicate whether or not a church is healthy? Give your thoughts.

2. What determines the health of a congregation?

3. Are you comfortable with the large church described in the chapter? Why, or why not?

4. Scripturally, is numerical growth normal for the church?

5. Can you explain the difference between management and leadership? What are the differences between these two functions given in this chapter?

6. Do you believe your congregation is over-managed?

7. Is your congregation under-led?

8. Over-managed congregations are in danger of becoming malignant rather than magnificent. True

or false _____. Give the reasoning for your answer.

9. Do you believe your congregation is being adversely affected by a controller or controllers?

10. Are you guilty of functioning as a controller? Take a close look at yourself and your leadership style before answering.

A VIEW FROM THE MIRRORS

—ɯ—

"Clichés are the closed doors of the comfortable."
(Bill Campbell)

Chapter Two

Considering the Angles

My wife Sue has always enjoyed laughing at the things I do. But one item tickling her funny bone is me in reference to my hair. You are really intrigued now, aren't you? Admit it. I knew you would be.

Allow me to explain a bit more of the hair issue with you. When Sue and I travel we try to stay in a motel where a well-angled mirror is available. The mirror allows me to see my hair from different vantage points. If I cannot see the sides or back portions of my hair I fear I will not have a well-groomed appearance. I always wish to look nice. I want every strand of hair I still possess to be in place. It is important for me to appear well groomed when I leave the motel room.

The author is not the only one who appreciates a well angled mirror. Women also enjoy having a correctly angled mirror when trying on a new dress. They want to see how the dress looks on them from a frontal position. But they also want to see the dress from side angles as well as rear angles. Seeing themselves from different perspectives is to see themselves in a complete way. It is a means of seeing the total picture in place of being restricted to a partial view.

The need for well-angled mirrors applies, as well, to the motorist. When traveling by vehicle, it is important to have your mirrors positioned correctly to see the various angles of the highway. Drivers even prefer to adjust their mirrors before they drive onto the highway. Blind spots may cause vision impairment and result in a fatal collision.

Mirrors are valuable tools. They provide the necessary angles for allowing persons to see well. Our lives would be severely handicapped without the benefit of mirrors.

Consider now the issue of clichés. Clichés are frequently used by persons of all ages and backgrounds. The author confesses he uses them too, and hears them used by others as well.

What are clichés? According to Webster, they are trite expressions. Stated in another way, clichés are overworked phrases. Because they are overused, they are well worn and lack freshness. The author often finds himself laughing at their repeated use. At other times he becomes intensely angry and impatient with their redundancy.

Clichés in the author's estimation resemble mirrors. A cliché is a mirror of sorts. For a cliché reveals a great deal about a person or group. They definitely provide an internal angle, and allow one to see what makes a person or group tick, just as a mirror provides an external view. Without clichés one would lack a needed mirror to adequately view people and their intentions.

Clichés are also used in congregational life by controlling church leaders and members. In fact, after having heard some of them used so often they have become a burr under the author's saddle. There is a tendency to see red when one of them is utilized. It is not even uncommon for the author to grit his teeth and experience a considerable degree of discomfort and frustration.

The experience with congregational clichés has led the author to engage in carrying a small pocket notebook. When a cliché is used, it is routinely jotted down. Recording the cliché serves to keep it fresh in mind and, helps as well, to recall it when a need exists to utilize it again.

Here is an opening cliché to unveil for observation. "If it ain't broke, don't fix it!" The implication in this cliché suggests things are okay as they presently exist in a church. Everything is okay because it has stood the test of time, and does not need to be tampered with, or, to be changed.

While an ounce of truth is in this cliché, it is not altogether correct. For a number of congregations using this cliché are on a plateau, and are experiencing numerical decline. They believe many things they do still work, but are in fact, no longer working. Thus, some things are clearly broken and are in need of repair.

Outdated methods are indeed no longer working. Yet, for some reason, these methods are still being perpetuated in congregations. New methods for doing ministry in the church today tend to be viewed with disdain and are resisted.

Consider the Clichés

But the clichés continue. There are several more needing to be highlighted. One cliché goes as follows, "making changes will divide our church." This cliché is used numerous times in congregational life.

Making changes, however, is no longer an optional matter. Changes are the norm rather than the exception. While this has not always been true, it is true today. Divisiveness may even erupt if changes are not made to lift an organization out of its predictable routine.

The author's oldest son Thom works for a structural engineering firm in Texas. One day I was discussing with him the reluctance many congregations have for making changes in the way they do church. This greatly surprised Thom. He indicated that each week his boss expects changes to occur in their engineering firm. In fact, Thom's boss becomes upset if changes do not occur. One's value as an employee in Thom's company is at stake if he or she is unwilling to make needed changes in the way they operate the engineering business.

Changes take place in all areas of life today. One major example relates to public places of business. These operations will rearrange their products. Nothing on the shelf will stay in the same place for long. Furthermore, restaurants are constantly offering their customers a changing menu, with an ever enlarged variety of entrees from which to choose.

Something caught the author's attention recently while staying in a motel. From six am until ten am this motel has long provided a continental breakfast for their guests. Some who stayed with them, however, indicated they did not have time to enjoy the breakfast provided in their dining room. Thus, they inquired, "could you provide a breakfast to take with us when we leave the motel?" As a result, the motel began preparing brown bag breakfasts for customers who needed their breakfast on the run.

This may sound strange. But businesses are learning they must constantly change to meet the needs and expectations of their customers. Motels will bend over backwards today to meet the needs of their guests. Change is not something optional, it is a necessity. They have also discovered excellent service is required if they are going to experience success as a motel chain.

Churches also need to make changes. This is necessary if the church is going to make a lasting difference in people's lives today. The changes, however, are not connected with changing the message of Scripture. For Scripture is not open to change. Yet, our methods for doing church are in constant need of being reshaped and updated.

An excellent example of my point is with the practice today of having two or more worship services. Some would argue only one worship service is needed, as one service has worked well for many years. Yet, congregations are discovering more than one worship service is required in order to meet a variety of needs.

Weekend work schedules and life's many demands, necessitate offering optional meeting times. Making this change is not an attempt to compromise and give people what they want. It is making sure the church is serving people's needs, in place of expecting people to conform to a congregation's rigid schedule.

Fearing change is the perpetrator of the next cliché. It follows the previous cliché, "making changes will divide our church." It goes this way, "we've never done it that way before." Have you heard this one? Surely you have. Some have chosen to label this cliché as, "the seven last words of the church."

This cliché is used because an attitude has developed in many congregations, in which anything new or different is under suspicion, and is predictably rejected. If it is an established practice, however, it is automatically considered acceptable in a church.

The foregoing thinking raises some red flags. Is something acceptable simply because it has been in existence for a while? Does its past history give it unquestioned protection today? It does not. But certain items have been maintained and placed in the realm of the untouchable in our churches. This kind of thinking has made the church an unhealthy place.

Consider a quick example. It concerns a couple wishing to be privately immersed. This was due to the husbands discomfort with going through a public baptismal service. The private baptismal request was okayed by the congregation's minister.

Yet, two controlling leaders of the church had a different view. The minister was informed, "we've never done it that way before. Baptisms here have always been performed on Sunday in our worship services."

Where is this expectation taught in Scripture? You will not find in Scripture where baptisms are performed only on Sunday, and at a public service of worship. Yet, many congregations have turned such matters into their own private interpretive turf. They have chosen to set the parameters on what is and what is not permissible.

The next cliché appears reasonable when it is first heard. But like the other clichés it crumbles once it has been considered at length. It goes this way, "we just need to work harder in our church right now." This appears to be a normal expectation. Certainly, some added effort would help to improve the present condition of any congregation.

This cliché is often used, for example, in regard to doing personal evangelism. "If we would just ring doorbells and make more personal home contacts, then our church would begin to grow again." At one time the foregoing thinking worked quite well. Congregations grew because its members were out in their communities ringing doorbells and making numerous contacts.

But communities are different today. What once worked well does not necessarily work well now. This definitely applies to home visitation. It is not acceptable as it once was. In fact, you may drive persons away from your church if you insist on making home visits. People appreciate their privacy. And the attempt to make evangelistic calls in their homes may do more harm than good.

Do not conclude, however, that making home visits is wrong. On occasions, a house call is in order. Yet, the timing must be right. And the timing will be right when one is invited to visit, or, when an appointment has been made. Badgering a neighborhood with cold evangelistic calls is not an advisable approach for a congregation to follow.

Someone has suggested, "we do not need to work harder, we need to work smarter." If one chooses to work smarter there are other ways to effectively engage people, and in the process, gain the evangelistic results anticipated.

Congregations choosing to look intently into the mirror of these clichés will receive needed insight. Specifically, they will become aware the clichés will serve to reveal many of the underlying problems promoting ill health in congregational life.

The author is still cautious about alluding to those individuals who utilize these clichés. Many using them are genuine and sincere in their intentions. They are attempting to do what they are convinced honors the Lord and promotes His cause. But the clichés used by congregations say much about them. They definitely reveal why a congregation is stuck in the mud and experiencing considerable ill health and decline.

Considering A Few More Clichés

As earlier indicated, there are many overworked clichés. They provide needed angles from which to view the church and its problems with controllers. As a congregation looks at itself through the mirror of clichés, it is prevented from falling into the unhealthy traps the clichés reveal. As a church sees what it should not be, it will help pave the way for understanding what a church should be.

When the various angles the clichés present are viewed a serious and sensitive issue will be recognized. Simply stated, they will portray congregations with which the reader is familiar. They may portray your own church. You may even see yourself as a perpetrator of a cliché.

Another cliché used in congregations is: "Our church isn't growing, but we want it to grow." This cliché suggests a congregation wishes to experience numerical growth. When it is heard a number of questions emerge.

- Are you sure you want your church to grow?
- How badly do you want your church to grow?
- Are you willing to make the necessary sacrifices for your church to grow?

- Are you even willing to pay some of the high prices required for your church to grow?

Important lessons have been learned from congregations utilizing this cliché. They are either declining, or, on a plateau. But they are unwilling to change their methods and the way they do church. This rigid posture lies at the center of their growth problems. Yet, they are unwilling to accept outside counsel, or, simply have not yielded to making the changes required to grow.

Perhaps an example would help to bring further clarification. Declining or plateaued congregations have a large number of older members attending their Sunday services. Yet, they have fewer younger members in attendance. These congregations insist they want to increase the number of younger persons. But they expect these individuals to enter their church and become like them. In other words, they expect younger members to accept:

- the same music;
- the same programs;
- the same methods;
- keep everything the way it has been for years.

You will not like what is going to be said next. This is especially true if you are connected with one of these congregations described. But when you go to a medical doctor for assistance, you will not like the diagnosis given there for alleviating your illness. Or, when attempting to lose weight you will not enjoy being told what you should and should not eat. Yet, to lose weight, or to get well, will require adherence to the diagnostician's expectations.

It is impossible, as well, for a church to grow and reach younger families without making the sacrifices required by a church diagnostician. A congregation must be receptive to making the necessary changes if it expects to achieve the growth desired.

The concern with growth could also be viewed in the following way. If you continue doing things the same way you have been doing them, then you should expect the same results. But if you are willing to make the needed changes you will experience numerical growth. You can continue talking about growing, yet it will only be idle talk unless you are willing to make the changes necessary to grow.

Allow the author to introduce another cliché. This is one more mirror giving the reader a picture of the problems with which many churches are faced. The cliché goes like this, "everyone today should have a voice in the church."

Did you catch the underlying suggestion here? It is indicating a church is a democracy. And in a democracy, all persons are expected to decide what a group of people will or will not do.

Some congregations believe a democratic process is biblical. They fail to understand, however, the church is not a democracy. The church is a theocracy. And a theocracy is not subservient to democratic thinking. God's will, and not the will of the people, is the agenda for action.

Knowing what those in a democracy think is helpful. But democratic thinking is not the base from which a congregation gets its bearings. Should this happen, a congregation is not functioning as it was designed by God to function.

It is unfortunate culture frequently defines how a church should carry out its mission. Culture wishes to view the church as a democracy, and not as a theocracy. Yet, nothing can be more divisive and misdirected than viewing a congregation as being, "of the people, by the people, and for the people."

Pope John Paul II has died. And his successor has been named. Pope Benedict the XVI is Pope John Paul II's successor. The media has projected the idea a majority of the populous believes Pope Benedict is not the right Pope for the present time. He is thought to be too rigid theologically for secular society. What is needed, according to the media, is a Pope more in touch with the needs and wishes of the people.

This raises some questions:

- Does a church exist to act in a manner in which society is pleased with its performance?

- Does secular society determine what a church should be or not be?

- Does society have the authority to shape the church according to its standards?

- Or, does the church have the responsibility to shape society according to God's standards?

The church exists to make a difference for God. It does not exist to respond to the changing whims of people. Being under a theocracy means God, and not society, determines the nature of the church and its actions. People are not over-looked in God's system, but society is expected to submit to God's standards, and should not insist upon having their own standards followed.

Consider another cliché. It goes like this: "A lot of people are upset right now in our church." Controlling lay persons will use this cliché to full advantage. It is one more example of church members perceiving a congregation to be a democracy. The expectation behind the cliché suggests the leadership of a local church is to be responsive to the wishes of its people.

This cliché places congregational leadership in a precarious position. For they understand the potential of division being set in motion by selfish members. Yet, they are also aware such a subtle tactic, as revealed by this cliché, threatens the health and well being of their church, and will hinder its growth. This divisive democracy, when poised against a congregation's leadership, resembles a dangerous snake coiled and ready to strike its cornered victim.

A question needing to be raised for these dissenters would be, "Who are these unhappy persons? Please name them." This approach forces the users of the cliché to rack their brain in pursuit of identifying available names. They will likely respond with the following, "well, they really do not want their names made known," or, "I can't name them all right now, but believe me they're out there!"

It will be discovered the one using the cliché is the real culprit. Any names this individual gives are generally of those he or she has incited. The person voicing this cliché is a master at acquiring adherents to buttress his or her cause.

Something else needs to be added here. When the user of the cliché is requested to name the persons who are upset, he or she will be placed in a defensive posture. Church leaders will not be the ones needing to establish a defense. Furthermore, church leaders will be placing themselves in a very healthy and pro-active position.

- Why do you think you need to communicate anything to those you say are unhappy?
- In fact, why must you choose to become an official mediator between members of the church and the congregation's leadership?

It is a dangerous role to assume as the result sets in motion congregational division. Do you want to encourage division in your church? Surely you or no one else would wish to create division.

The cliché among all the others troubling the author most is the next one. This cliché concerns him because the person using it fails to see the arrogant role he or she has chosen to assume. The cliché goes like this, "I really believe that I need to save my church."

Can you believe anyone would choose to make this statement? Yet, it has been used effectively today by many controlling churchmen. Here are some questions that emerge when this cliché is used:

- Is there more than one Savior needed in a church?
- How can there be two or more?
- Does the church need to be saved again by anyone? Isn't once enough?
- How can a person place himself or herself in a position that calls for messianic abilities? For a person to make this claim is to place him or herself in an unauthorized position.

Those who use this cliché, however, would be prepared to defend themselves. The defense would go as follows: "The church is under attack today by evil forces! You would agree, wouldn't you? Doesn't the church need to be defended? Besides, if I don't do it, who else will?"

The church needs no special representative to defend it. It definitely needs no defending from someone setting him or herself up as its protective messiah.

The church does, however, need members who will model the teachings of Jesus. And it needs members, as well, who will engage in the mission of disciple making. It is sad the church has been inundated today with numerous controllers, yet few who are willing to actively serve in the ministry of making disciples.

Here is another cliché to consider. This one is used by a congregation wishing to identify a scapegoat for its failures. It is expressed with the following words: "Everything would be okay in our church right now if we just had the right preacher." Have you heard it before?

Controlling churchmen have used this cliché for years. They have used the cliché to justify the ineffectiveness of their congregation by the removal of any blame from themselves. The more troubling aspect, however, is the Lord's mission suffers in the aftermath from the subtle use of this cliché. A host of congregations, along with their ministers, have been destroyed through its use.

It is the author's conviction controlling churchmen are destroying churches today! Congregations are daily closing their doors.[6] Ministers are being driven out of leadership ministry. And when preaching ministers are lost, congregations remove one of the most valuable assets it possesses.

One leadership minister's story needs to be shared. This minister worked to rescue a dying congregation. Headway was being made. Advancement was occurring until some controlling churchmen in the congregation joined forces to have him removed.

Opposition centered on unhappiness with his efforts to make "unauthorized changes," in their church. A petition was set in motion to have him removed as the congregation's leadership minister. In two short months enough hate and discontent had been engendered against him to put this minister and his family out on the street. The success of their actions fueled these words: "Our congregation needs the right minister. And Brother Joe just wasn't the right man for our church. We needed to have him removed."

But Brother Joe's dismissal did not really help the church. While he was not thought to be the right minister, the church has resumed a downward spiral. Any day now the church will be forced to close its doors. Yet, the church was convinced, "everything would be okay in our church right now if we just had the right preacher." But is this church really okay? Will it ever be okay again?

Here is another troubling item that cannot be ignored. Brother Joe was removed as the congregation's leadership minister. He has also left congregational ministry. In fact, he has given up on the institutional church. He is one more minister who has been pierced with the devils arrows, or, one of the devil's controlling clichés. The devil is having a hay day in many of our congregations! He is utilizing a minority of unhealthy and controlling church members to reek havoc and destruction.

There is certain to be a critic or two at this point. Predictably, these critics will respond in the following way:

- "Is it always members in the church who are guilty?"
- "Aren't ministers just as guilty as members of the church in creating congregational ill health?"

We do have a number of unhealthy ministers. But the failure of congregations to grow today can be attributed largely, not to unhealthy ministers, but to the presence of unhealthy controllers. Though small in number they represent a formidable and dedicated squad. This devilish contingent is engaged in suffocating the life out of numerous congregations in America. We need to probe the problem further in the next chapter.

Reflections

1. The author utilizes clichés in this chapter as windows through which to view a congregational controller. How do the clichés given enable one to see the controller in action?

2. Which one of the clichés have you heard used more frequently in your church? Give the particular context in which you have experienced the use of this cliché.

3. Established or traditional congregations encounter problems when changes are proposed. Why do changes create problems in traditional churches?

4. Are there limits to making changes in congregational life? Explain.

5. How do you think congregations can become more effective in doing evangelism? Do congregations need to do evangelism the way it has always been done?

6. Are congregations saying they want to grow always willing to pay the prices required to grow? Give your answer after prayerful thought.

7. Congregations are taught in Scripture to function as a theocracy. Does your church function as a theocracy or democracy? How are the two different?

8. The author made reference to "protective messiahs" in a congregation. Is this a problem in your church? Give an example.

9. Does your church have a history of short ministerial tenure? Why?

10. Has the practice of having short ministerial tenure been a healthy experience for your church?

PROBING THE PROBLEM

—⚭—

"A lighthouse shines for others - not for itself."
(Author unknown)

Chapter Three

Problems Now

The author remembers reading a story about an old lighthouse. It was situated on a dangerous rocky shoreline overlooking a vast sea of water. Through the years the lighthouse had been a noted bastion of strength in helping save shipwrecked passengers who had crashed on its rugged coastline.

Yet, its staff decided one day they needed to make some changes with the old lighthouse. They needed to fix up the facilities and give it an appealing appearance. In short, they were tired of seeing the lighthouse as a bad eyesore.

The project was eventually approved and completed. The lighthouse was a beautifully remodeled facility. But once the effort had been completed, a radical change was noted in the lighthouse staff. They had a beautiful facility, but little was being done in regard to saving lives. For the staff had transformed the lighthouse into an exclusive club. No longer was there interest in saving the victims who had crashed on their rugged coastline. They were now more concerned with their elite club and keeping the remodeled facility untainted by dirty, bleeding, and smelly people.

You can imagine the end of this story, can't you? Shipwrecks continued to take place on those rugged coastal waters. In fact, the number of shipwrecks dramatically increased. Yet, no one was being saved.

Can you imagine that? What had happened? Simply stated, the little lighthouse had lost its reason for existence. They were no longer devoted to saving hurting and drowning people. Their purpose was lost in the midst of institutional glut and selfishness. They were suffering from amnesia, a word the author introduced earlier.

There is a need to shift gears at this point. Thinking needs to be turned in the direction of the church. What happened to the old lighthouse has also happened to churches. For various reasons congregations have ceased functioning in a biblical fashion.

They have lost their way. They have lost a sense of who and what they were called to be. Spiritual amnesia has occurred. And nothing is more pathetic than an organization, whether church or secular, that has become confused and disoriented in regard to its purpose. It can no longer meet the needs of hurting people. Instead, it reverts to having people serve it and fulfill its institutional needs.

Keep in mind the original intention of the lighthouse. It existed to function as a life-saving station. But the lighthouse made a tragic mistake when it ceased being a rescue operation and chose to become an elite club.

Think about this scenario a bit more. The Lord designed the church to be His life saving station on earth's rugged coastline. In fact, the church is not only intended to be a life-saving station, it is also designed to offer continued assistance to those who have been rescued. A church is not designed for civic club purposes, or, to be an elite social organization for its members. It exists for the needs of others.

Congregations losing their way share another trait with the lighthouse. In the process of making a change in their mission they moved from the lighthouse meeting the needs of others to meeting their own needs. Everything became focused on the interests of the lighthouse staff and its crew.

They had evolved into an elite huddle of persons in which the members were allowed to enjoy a serene social life in the club.

The problem just described has also invaded the life of many congregations today. Rather than existing for the needs of the world, congregations have chosen to turn inward and have lavished undue concern upon themselves.

Perhaps a careful rereading of John 3:16 would be most helpful at this point. For the concern God has in this verse is with the world. There is no mention here of the church being His major concern. Rather, He is focused upon the hurting, bleeding, sick and dying on earth's rugged coastline outside the safe confines of the lighthouse.

This is a tough issue to face. No one wishes to admit they are confused and misdirected. But an ailment or malady cannot be effectively corrected unless persons are first willing to face their problem. They are, in fact, sick. And the amnesia here identified is an ingrown sickness. For congregations to overcome the ailment will involve the acknowledgment they have become unhealthy, as they have developed into a holy huddle.

There are various ways the author has been sensitized to an in-grown congregation. In one church a minister pointed out the limited parking area around their facility. Even on normal Sunday mornings few parking slots were available for late arrivers. Recognizing a holiday Sunday was approaching the minister urged his leaders to park their cars across the street in an adjacent parking lot.

The minister thought very little about making the request, believing it would be well received. "Showing concern for visitors," he reasoned, "is a courtesy any congregation would wish to extend." Yet, are you sure this is the way the leaders of his church felt, and even the way the majority of churches and their leaders feel today? Have you ever brought a simple request like this one to the attention of the leadership in your church?

The minister said three or four leaders in the meeting responded with sharp resentment. They said to him: "Why should we be expected to park so far away from our entrance doors? This church is ours! It belongs to us! We've paid for it! Why shouldn't the strangers who rarely attend be expected to park across the street and walk back across to our services?"

How does the foregoing response come across to you? Does it bring you pain? Is it possibly a scene you have already experienced in your church? Would you say this congregation was demonstrating the club mentality of the lighthouse staff and crew? Is your church now suffering from this same kind of clubhouse mentality?

Consider another scene. A congregation was growing in number. In fact, so many people were being attracted to the congregations worship services several families were suggesting an additional worship service be added. From the ministers perspective this seemed a reasonable request. Thus, he shared the idea at the congregations next scheduled board meeting.

You should have been in the meeting when the idea was introduced. One veteran board member listened to the minister's suggestion. Yet, he could not agree with the minister's reasoning. His response followed: "I've been a member of this congregation for thirty-one years. We've always had one worship service here. Why should we now compromise and give people what they want?"

The author laughed when he heard this response. It is interesting the church leader did not see his personal compromise being played out. For compromise can work in both directions. The church leader indicated he did not want to make a compromise and give people what they wanted.

Yet, he expected others to compromise and practice public worship the way he wanted it to be done.

The issue with the foregoing church leader is not with compromise. Rather, he is concerned with exercising control. It was an established practice to have one worship service. He did not want to let go of his traditional comfort zone. In short, he was not willing to entertain the idea of two services, or, to change the way things had always been done in his church. Does this also strike you as being a sort of clubhouse mentality church?

There are other ways in which the church has evolved into an exclusive club, much like the lighthouse gang, described earlier. For one thing, a number of congregations display a wide variety of **programs.** And church members are expected to participate in these activities. Traditional programs have attained considerable importance in many established congregations today.

A number of problems are associated with church programs. One problem is that the majority of people in a congregation no longer actively participate in them. They have chosen not to participate because they do not see the programs as contributing to their spiritual development. Yet, the programs are continued, and more it seems, out of habit or tradition than anything else.

Church programs are also continued because nothing worthwhile has been deemed necessary to replace them. Churchmen believe a continuation of these programs will help keep their members from losing interest. As members engage in various church activities, it is thought, they will be less likely to drop out of the life of the church organization or club.

Another problem connected with maintaining church programs is the reason or reasons congregations have them. In other words, are they achieving anything worthwhile? Do they, for example, serve to enhance the spiritual life of the members in any way? Will they become stronger Christian disciples through participating in these programs? If not, why have them?

Sometimes church members groan over the fact they are faced with another church program to attend. Church programs wear out church members. This is but one more of the serious symptoms of sickness with which congregations are faced today.

Another problem regarding the practice of perpetuating church programs is the time involved in conducting them.

They are time consuming. And a person's time is increasingly guarded. Why? Because people consider their time as being among the most precious of all the commodities of life they possess.

Have you ever stopped to note the large number of church programs on a congregation's calendar of monthly activities? These programs are conducted primarily for the members. Church guests or newer members have little, if any, understanding of why a church even has them.

The church may also be noted as being a club in the way certain **people** are elevated above others. In other words, congregations are guilty of giving some church members greater attention than they do other members in their fellowship. What these favored people say and think even carries greater weight in a congregation's decision making process.

The practice of elevating certain persons in congregational life has been made clear in another way. Specifically, church members will refer to someone in their church as being a, "good Christian." This expression suggests some Christians are, "good," whereas other Christians are "mediocre" or, "bad." While no one using this terminology, "good Christian," would choose to agree with the thinking here, this

71

kind of descriptive rhetoric is offensive and downgrading to many members of a congregation.

It is also important to recognize Scripture does not encourage the practice of highlighting some Christians over others. In fact, showing preference indicates a congregation has drifted from its basic Christian moorings.

James addresses this issue squarely when he corrects those who would choose to practice partiality (James 2:1-4). A church showing favoritism, according to James, gives evidence of having lost its way. In short, it is suffering from a form of spiritual illness, as it practices the clubhouse mentality.

In addition to people and programs causing a church to become unhealthy, insisting everything be done in a rigid **procedural** fashion can also impact a church in adverse ways. Many have learned this is one of the biggest problems faced by established congregations. It has especially become a major source of disappointment to a congregation's newer members. Once they unite with a church they are shocked to discover it is burdened with an unbelievable number of rules and regulations members are expected to follow.

A major example relates to the existence of church by-laws. In many congregations a set of by-laws has become a heavy and binding yoke around its neck. Some churches possess a set of by-laws very tome like in appearance. As an added note, these congregations are frequently more attentive to the requirements in their by-laws than the teaching of Scripture.

Along with church by-laws are also additional manuals of procedure. These are further elaborations of how members may or may not function in a congregation. Some congregations have established so many written regulations it is virtually impossible to keep up with all the expectations in these documents. It often reminds the author of the growing number of laws enacted in our country the average citizen knows very little if anything about.

Problems Then

Dysfunctional congregations abound today. Hopefully, this fact has been well established. Congregations were nonetheless dysfunctional during biblical times. The foregoing is evident when the New Testament is read with a discerning eye.

Frequently we hear comments about the need to become a New Testament church. But which congregation in the New

Testament would you prefer to be like? Is there a congregation portrayed in Scripture more preferable to another one? For example, would you want to be like the congregations displayed in Rome or Corinth in order to be labeled a healthy church body?[7] Are congregations in Scripture free from the problems associated with ill health?

While reading the New Testament it is clear church health has not been achieved by these first century congregations. In fact, the opposite is true. It is amazing to observe the plethora of church problems emerging within the life of the first century church. Consider a sampling of these problems through a brief analysis of the New Testament.

- Several persons have become drunk when the Lord's Supper is shared at congregational gatherings (see I Corinthians 11:17-34).

- Serious divisions within a congregation have become upsetting to its founding minister (see I Corinthians 1:10-11).

- Serious racial tension makes for uneasy congregational relationships (see Romans and Ephesians 2:14-22).

- An individual named Diotrephes functions as a controller. He plays power games in the church (see III John 9).

- A group known as Judaizers placed heavy rules and regulations upon Christian believers. Grace was not sufficient as more was thought to be required in order to become acceptable to God (see Galatians 3).

- A young man in one congregation was living a sexually open life with his stepmother. The church accepted and even bragged about this unhealthy relationship (see I Corinthians 5:1-8).

- Congregations were guilty of practicing favoritism or partiality toward significant persons attending their meetings (see James 2:1-13).

- A congregation was condemned because it had completely forsaken Christian love (see Revelation 2:1-7).

- Another congregation was guilty of compromising with false teaching (see Revelation 2:12-17).

- A congregation allowed a Jezebel to introduce pagan practices into its life (see Revelation 2:18-29).

- One church was extremely arrogant and engaged in bragging about its past reputation (see Revelation 3:1-6).

- Another church was condemned for its apathetic or lukewarm condition (Revelation 3:14-22).

- Some congregations were guilty of allowing false teachers to promote their heresy. One major example of false teaching stressed Jesus did not come to earth as a human (1 John 4:2-3).

- There were even some Christian leaders who were unable to get along and work together. Paul and Barnabas serve as a case in point. They had a serious disagreement among them regarding John Mark. Their disagreement resulted in the two leaders separating and going different directions (see Acts 15:36-41).

Is the foregoing information sufficient to convince the reader congregational problems are not isolated to the twenty-first century? Hopefully, this brief biblical survey has revealed numerous dysfunctional problems faced by first century congregations. While the problems faced were different from those problems faced by congregations today, there were nonetheless numerous dysfunctional practices.

Recognizing congregational dysfunction in the first century is very important. For there is a tendency to read the Scriptures ideally, or with rose colored glasses. Persons want to believe what took place in biblical times was, unlike today, perfect. But, this brief survey reveals the foregoing thought to be a false idea or notion. The persons and congregations portrayed in Scripture also faced serious health problems in church life, much like individuals face in congregational life today.

Reflections

1. Why do congregations become more focused on themselves than they do on others?

2. Does your congregation have a clubhouse mentality? If so, give an example of the clubhouse mentality at work in your church.

3. How can the congregational clubhouse mentality be overcome?

4. Do you view church programs as being beneficial? Explain.

5. Why do congregations elevate some members above other members?

6. Have your by-laws become a problem for your church? Please explain.

7. If by-laws have created problems for your church, how could the problems be surmounted?

8. Are you able to share other examples of dysfunction in the life of congregations portrayed in Scripture, and not addressed in this chapter?

9. How do you think the **leaders** of a church should respond to dysfunctional problems in congregational life?

10. How do you think the **members** of a church should respond to dysfunctional problems in congregational life?

OFFERING SOME SOLUTIONS

—๛—

*"One definition of insanity is to believe
that you can keep doing what you've been doing
and get different results."
(Anonymous)*

*"I've learned that life challenges us with the fact
that everything can be done better."
(Anonymous)*

Chapter Four

Realigning Attitudes

Problems in congregational life are clearly abundant. And their presence is why individuals go to theologians, ministers, and Christian educators to seek answers. These experts are not consulted, however, to simply talk about problems. There is a desire to find solutions.

When congregations face problems some options are open to them.

- They can ignore their problems.
- They can live with their problems.
- They can talk about their problems.
- They can seek to work through their problems.
- They can look for outside help.

In other words, they can search for a ministry practitioner to assist them. This book is an endeavor to offer congregations some outside help.

A basic problem plaguing congregations is in the area of attitudes. The initial attempt on the part of the author was to focus the reader's attention on a congregations core values. Specifically, what does a congregation believe? Yet, congregations are often thinking correctly about what they believe, but they still seem to be stuck in the mud. They are unable to make headway or progress even though their core beliefs have been established.

Why is the foregoing true? Because even though a congregation is thinking clearly about its doctrinal beliefs, does not always mean it is acting correctly. A congregation is frequently stuck because of its flawed attitudes.

Attitudes refer to the way a congregation's actions are perceived by those who observe them. And a congregation's attitudes are as crucial to their witness as what they believe. Poor attitudes will serve to stifle a congregation's growth and make it an unhealthy fellowship.

An example can be provided with which to illustrate the foregoing point. A long pursued serial killer has been captured. When arrested it was discovered he was a very devoted husband and father, as well as a responsible wage earner for his family. Furthermore, he was an active and prominent leader in his local church, including serving for several years as a community scout leader.

Yet, this man was living a dual life. He was not only a respected citizen, he was also a serial killer. He claimed to believe many important things, yet he lived a life denying his core values. How can you claim to love God, for example, yet not value another person's life? He lived a lie as his actions did not follow his core values.

The same thing happens in congregations. There is no suggestion being made here that persons in congregations are serial killers. But the actions which flow from peoples attitudes often destroy their belief system.

Congregations, for example, stress they believe in God, in Jesus Christ, the Holy Spirit, and in the Scriptures. Yet, they nonetheless appear to others as being negative and mean-spirited. If you do not view everything the way they do, you are immediately attacked and criticized.

Ask the following questions. Would Jesus act in a way that was unloving, unkind, and unforgiving? Would the Holy Spirit encourage someone to be unloving, unkind, and unforgiving? Yet, church members will often use the Bible and their personal beliefs as a hammer with which to pound people into believing what they want them to believe.

Nothing is wrong with having strong beliefs. Yet, to become harsh and mean-spirited with what one believes, places serious doubts in peoples minds about the genuineness of ones walk with Christ. Additionally, it hinders the ability of a local congregation to be a strong and healthy community witness.

In an earlier chapter the author shared some of the clichés revealing the harsh and insensitive attitudes perpetuated in congregations. Pondering these clichés would help sensitize church members to the dysfunctional ways in which congregations become wrongly focused today. To see these clichés in operation will help enable believers to move to a renewed level of commitment within congregational life.

The reason undesirable attitudes develop in churches relates to how persons view the church and their participation in it. Life in a congregation is more often than not a connection to a church, and is not a vital connection with Christ. As a result, the church is viewed as a place where religious business is conducted. The church is not viewed as a place for prayer, nourishment in the Scriptures, and for having genuine Christian fellowship and community outreach.

In what ways though can congregations realign their dysfunctional attitudes and actions today?

- A good place to begin is to allow themselves to be highly sensitized to the nature of the problem. The author has sought to achieve this sensitizing process through the foregoing insights and thoughts. If a congregation has been challenged to take a more careful look at its life and witness, then the effort here has been successful.

- Attitudes can also be realigned when members of a congregation begin a serious relationship with Christ. This is a crucial step in ones spiritual development. For through a serious relationship with Christ Jesus, members of a congregation are able to move beyond a simple attachment to a religious organization to a vital and intimate connection with Christ.

Restoring Passion

Attitude realignment is essential. A second area of turn-around needed today is with the restoration of passion. This word should not be associated with romance or sex, although there is a tendency to associate the word with strong expressions of sexual eroticism.

The use of the word in this volume is much different. Passion refers to an intense emotion. It is especially powerful when expressed through ones fervor for Christ.

Passion is a quality needed by all Christians. For without passion there is an absence of spiritual energy. A serious concern exists today in congregations regarding the growing loss of spiritual passion in church life.

Some time ago a movie was produced entitled, *The Sixth Sense*. The star of the movie was Bruce Willis. While drawn to Willis' strong performance, the author was more greatly captivated by the role of a young boy making one unforget-table statement. He said: "I see dead people." The boy was not deluded, nor had he lost his eyesight. He was actually seeing dead people around him. Yet, he was still among the living.

As a participant in congregational life the author has a deep affinity with this boy. He can see dead people also. Not dead humans like the boy saw in the movie. Rather, the dead people the author sees are those in congregations today. They are dead because they have lost their passion. They no longer possess the enthusiasm and zeal they once had. They have become calloused, frozen, and paralyzed. When a Christian loses his or her spiritual passion this person simply shrivels up and dies. One comes to resemble a dead or lifeless corpse.

Predictably, Christians possess passion at the beginning of their Christian walk. Time, however, has a way of numbing them to their initial excitement. Time also causes them to lose the spiritual momentum and driving power for dynamic Christian living.

The author has experienced occasional losses of passion in his ministry. The experience has produced times of extreme despondency. Furthermore, acquiring the help needed to snap out of this paralyzing condition was most difficult.

The loss of passion has also been witnessed in the lives of other Christians. They were once vibrant and afire for Christ. To be in their presence was to enjoy an unforgettable experience. Yet, following their downward spiral, they appeared defeated, dead, and lifeless.

Even other leadership ministers who were once powerful instruments in God's hands have become pale corpses following the loss of their passion. Their devotion and excitement brought others joy. But their disappointment in leading dysfunctional churches has left them as powerless and lifeless corpses. Many of these passionless ministers have left leadership ministry altogether.

Congregations are meant to be vibrant organisms. Yet, nothing is more disheartening than to see a congregation without passion. It is a depressing source of disappointment to those who participate in its life, and for those, as well, who observe its lifeless and cold form. Having a passionless church body is one of the greatest sources for having unhealthy congregations in our time.

A model example of passions power comes to mind. Our family was enjoying a wonderful vacation in the Ozarks of Missouri. We stayed one of the nights in a rather quaint motel. Early the next morning our middle son Mike awakened before the rest of the family, and chose to go outside and look around. In a matter of minutes Mike was back inside our motel room. He was more excited than I ever remember seeing him. His eyes were huge and dancing. He was talking so fast we could hardly understand what he was trying to say. Mike was simply breathless and overjoyed.

Immediately, he opened his one hand and revealed a wad of money. We noted he had several bills and some change. Needless to say, Mike thought he had discovered a massive treasure. We cautioned Mike that someone may step forward and claim the money. Mike had no plans, however, of releasing his treasure.

Reflecting on Mike's experience has caused me to wonder. Specifically, why do we often lack a passionate response like Mike's as a body of Christians? Why is there an attitude of religious business as usual, or, simply going through religious motions? In short, why is the excitement Mike demonstrated frequently absent in congregational life? Have we lost passion? Isn't discovering the Lord more exciting than the discovery of money?

Believers need to catch the contagious spirit conveyed by one of the parables of Jesus. It reads this way: "Again, the kingdom of heaven is like treasure hidden in a field, which a man found and hid; and for joy over it he goes and sells all that he has and buys that field" (Matthew 13:44).

Obviously, this treasure surpassed in worth all other material items this unnamed man had owned during his lifetime. Thus, when he discovered this treasure, he was willing to give up everything in order to make it his own.

The scene revealed in this parable was not an uncommon one in biblical times. For those having possessions would often bury their treasures before departing on a journey. Banks or savings institutions were non-existent. The ground became the major safe deposit box for one's valuables.

The treasure portrayed in Matthew's gospel was very unique. For nothing the man possessed was considered too valuable to release in order to purchase this field. It was a treasure with which he was overjoyed, and passionate about possessing.

To be able to identify Christ as ones Savior and Lord should also ignite great passion. He is much more precious than money discovered in a motel parking lot, or, even in a field. Christ is the greatest of all earthly treasures, as finding Him enables a person to connect with eternity.

Time and distance often serve, however, to blunt this initial passion for Christians. What are some of the causes of passion being lost?

- High on the list of reasons for the loss of passion is the spiritual condition of the local church. When a church loses its passion it becomes a spiritual drain on those connected with it.
- Another reason persons lose their passion relates to the world around them. The things of earth, visible as they are, become much easier to embrace, as they make an immediate appeal to ones senses.
- Passion is also lost through a failure to continue in the development of ones personal relationship with the Lord. He is not someone you discover one day and lay aside the next. One needs to intensify the relationship through daily Bible study, prayer, fellowship, and service.
- One more reason passion is absent relates to the level of ones reservoir of trust. When your faith is running low it will result in spiritual excitement being squeezed out of you. The diminished character of faith eventually equates to one being unable to practice the level of faith being discussed in the next point.

Risking It

A third needed turnaround for congregations is in the area of taking risks. Congregations willing to step out and act on the basis of their faith are examples of a risk taking fellowship. Many congregations are unwilling to make this crucial step. They have chosen to respond to what they are able to see, or, they think is humanly possible to achieve.

When viewed from a human perspective, the foregoing approach is understandable. For no one wishes to place his or her church in a precarious position by way of risky decision making. If the end result cannot be seen up front, many congregations are unwilling to take the uncertain step of faith.

From a spiritual perspective, however, Christians do not walk by sight. Rather, they are called upon to conduct their lives by faith. The role of faith for believers makes risk taking unavoidable. Scripture teaches, "For, we walk by faith, and not by sight" (II Corinthians 5:7).

There is the need to be clear about the nature of faith. To possess faith is more than saying one believes in God. James reveals the impotence of this kind of faith when he points out that the demons acknowledge God exists, and they even tremble or shudder at this awareness (James 2:19). If one only says he or she believes in God, it is not actually a faith willing to take risks.

What is being suggested here by faith is much different. Faith is a virtue leading one to act in accordance with what he or she says is believed. Thus, scriptural faith is not something passive. Rather, faith is an active quality. It is a virtue propelling one to act outside the box, or, to go beyond what is humanly reasoned as being possible or achievable.

This reminds the author of a story. It is about a circus tightrope walker. He was ready to perform before an excited crowd in a huge tent. As he prepares to walk onto the tightrope he begins to communicate with his audience. He asks the audience if they believe he can walk across the tightrope without falling. They cheer him on with great confidence, believing he can walk across it successfully. Their confidence in his ability is rewarded by his successful walk across the tightrope.

He then introduces the audience to his cycle. He wants to know if they believe he can ride the cycle across the tightrope without falling. A loud cheer of confidence for the tightrope walker roars throughout the tent. He balances himself and begins his ride to the other side. Arriving onto the opposite platform safely his audience has their confidence rewarded once again, and the noise of their excitement is deafening.

But the tightrope walker was not through yet. Calling a beautiful young lady to his side, he wants to know if the audience believes he can ride his cycle across the tightrope with this young lady perched on his shoulders. Shouts and cheers of confidence rise from the crowd. And again, he achieves his daring feat. The audience is thrilled with his abilities and theatrics.

A final daring act remained. Facing the audience he asks them the question,"how many believe I can ride this cycle across the tightrope with one of you riding on my shoulders?" The shouts and cheers rose to an even louder crescendo.

Facing the crowd the tightrope walker questions his onlookers with these frightening words, "which one of you wants to be the one to ride on my shoulders?" Suddenly there was a hush over the audience. There were no takers.

The obvious point of this story is that faith requires risk. The crowd said they believed the tightrope walker could achieve each of the challenges he placed before them. But, in the last and most daring challenge of all, they were unable to accept the risk of attempting to ride to the other side on his shoulders.

Congregations are much like this circus crowd. For their internal beliefs do not always match their outward actions. This weakness in faith is why we have many unhealthy congregations today. A restoration to a healthy faith is necessary if a congregation is going to be able to practice what it believes.

With the foregoing thoughts in mind the eleventh chapter of Hebrews needs some careful consideration. This chapter has been correctly labeled, "God's Hall of Fame," or, "God's Hall of Faith." It portrays a number of persons willing to take a risk, and to step out on what they believed. The end was not clearly in view. Yet, they were willing to accept the challenge of relying on God to reward their faith.

Such action is required to please God (see Hebrews 11:6). For apart from having a faith willing to risk it, there can be no genuine connection with Him. Faith is the umbilical cord attaching one to the Lord. When He instructs anyone to do something, a person does it because he or she possesses a confident faith. Further questions are unnecessary. Added discussion will only result in removing the expectation out of the realm of faith.

As one reads the eleventh chapter of Hebrews, he or she will see revealed the names of several persons who acted solely on the basis of their faith. These biblical personalities serve as key examples for those who wish to please God through a faithful life of risk taking. When faced with risk, it is important to have models to inspire persons on life's journey. These models are now in heaven's grandstands cheering persons on to victory as they also take risks in the present day arena of faith (see Hebrews 12:1-2).

Some questions need to be posed at this point:

- Will your church be remembered for its faithful actions?
- Will you be remembered as a person of faith in your church for making a difference during your lifetime?
- Or, will persons look back and remember you and your church as being among those choosing to follow their own agenda in place of following Gods risk taking agenda?
- Will you be remembered as a church known for its fighting and feuding?
- Or, will you be among the elite band who has sought to achieve the victories of faith God provides those willing to risk all for Him?

The Hebrew writer sets forth an important reminder for the Christian: "But without faith it is impossible to please Him, for he who comes to God must believe that he is, and that he is a rewarder of those who diligently seek Him" (Hebrews 11:6).

Choosing to risk it all will require some big shoulders. It is no simple task to step out and do something for God when it appears impossible to be achieved.

Children can help teach a vital lesson here. They have learned to depend upon their parents for their needs. And their dependence is amply rewarded by loving parents who take care of them in a parent's special way. If parents care for their children should we not much more be led to rely upon our heavenly Father to take care of us?

Escaping "Churchianity"

There is a need, beyond risking it, to keep the church focused on Christianity. This is necessary as many congregations have chosen to replace Christianity with churchianity. In other words, they demonstrate a greater concern for the church than they do for Christ. Churchianity has been responsible for bringing much harm to the cause of

Christ in the present time. It has resulted in the church being unable to provide an effective witness to those searching for spiritual truth.

Yet, while spiritual seekers continue to be skeptical of religious organizations, they have not forsaken their spiritual aspirations. Persons are living in one of the most spiritually sensitive times in history. But many congregations are missing out on this growing spiritual openness. The foregoing failure has caused these churches to become increasingly ineffective in their outreach. It has also resulted in their inability to grow and enjoy a quality life together.

One glaring evil spawned by churchianity has been a strong and growing resistance to "institutional" or "established" churches.[8] Bare in mind while many are open spiritually, the spiritually sensitive are not open to the superficial religious institutions around them. In fact, the spiritually open tend to reject churches today as being unworthy of their time and devotion.

One is led to think churches would be the most likely place on earth in which to encounter spirituality. But the spiritually open believe established congregations today resemble the culture more than they resemble Christ.

A number of individuals in our culture even see the church as being composed of those who have joined a religious club, or, organization. Reggie McNeal sees this happening when he writes: "In North America the invitation to become a Christian has largely become an invitation to convert to the church."[9] McNeal's view is on target as today's church has largely lost the dynamic image portrayed by the first century church.

A refusal to accept institutions, however, does not mean spirituality is non-existent. Rather, individuals have turned to those sources they believe are spiritual, and who will, in turn, assist them in their spiritual quest. Throughout history persons have demonstrated a passionate need for spirituality. When it is not available in a church, they will search for it elsewhere.

Secular bookstores have numerous volumes on their shelves addressing spirituality. A majority of these volumes are not Judaeo-Christian. Yet, their existence suggests people today are open to spirituality. This is a significant indicator for congregations focused on growing. It is nonetheless a sign society is spiritually healthy. Congregations must recover their own spiritual roots if they are going to be able to reach the spiritually hungry of this age.

Several important results will follow when congregations regain genuine spirituality:

- Recovering spirituality will be the necessary spark for igniting passion in congregational life.
- Recovering spirituality will help bring genuine character to church membership.
- Recovering spirituality will also be the important step toward providing a valid Christian witness to communities and the larger world.
- And, recovering spirituality will, in the end, achieve the goal of acquiring congregational health, and will help achieve evangelistic growth.

Another important issue to consider is how a congregation goes about escaping the disease of "churchianity." How does it recapture Christianity? The foregoing question is a matter of concern for church leaders today confronted with the problem of congregational ill health.

A congregation will not be able to recapture Christianity by working itself up into an emotional frenzy. Nor will Christianity be recovered as a church attempts to achieve a high level of moral commitment. There is not a magic potion available guaranteeing the setting in motion of spirituality in congregational life.

So, how can spirituality be recovered? A good point at which to begin is to direct attention toward Scripture. In the opening three chapters of Revelation some helpful instruction is provided.

Attention needs to be focused on the Ephesian church in this section of Scripture (see Revelation 2:1-7). The fourth verse addresses the congregation's central problem. They are condemned with the words, "you have left your first love."

Several interpretations have been given to offer clarification for the meaning of this phrase. One interpretation stands out above the others. Jesus is telling this church they do not love Him the way they once did. At one time their love for Christ was red-hot. Yet, the original intensity is now absent. They were not in danger of losing their love for Him, it had already occurred.

This word picture portrays many congregations up to this day. They are busy, as verses two and three indicate. Yet, what appears on the outside is but a shell, as what is on the inside does not match with what is on the outside. They have allowed themselves to evolve into a mere religious club. A serious relationship with the Lord is lacking.

Someone has suggested "you cannot give to others what you do not possess." And many congregations suffer today from being unable to give anything spiritual to persons of our time. They are unable to do so because they no longer possess it to give away. They have lost their first love. A club mentality has replaced a red-hot love relationship with the Lord.

One will even notice in many congregations a lot of attention is being given to traditional programs, important people, and rigid procedural practices. But the serious observer will soon wonder about the meaning of these activities. In short, do they have anything at all to do with a church being a fellowship of committed Christians?

The church is called to glorify God as it grows in Christian discipleship, and as it engages in making disciples. When the foregoing is not happening, a church has departed from its first love.

But once again, how does a church escape "churchianity" and return to Christianity? Jesus gives a three-fold prescription in verse five for making this turnaround.

- **Prescription # 1 -** *"Remember"* - The foundational step for returning to the roots of Christianity is to be found in the disciplined use of ones mind: "Remember therefore from where you have fallen." Christianity is not a mere intellectual affair. Yet, there is nonetheless a need for a congregation to make the mental journey of retracing its steps back to Christ. This journey will include an emotional response. But the journey will also involve a clear and renewed understanding and awareness of God's demonstrated love. A church is in poor health spiritually when it fails to engage in this act of remembering from where it has fallen.

- **Prescription # 2 - *"Repent"*** - Remembering is not enough. It is but the beginning. Along with a retracing of a congregations steps back to Christ is the additional need of repentance. Repentance is a strong biblical word calling a church to a radical life change. The change called for is a transition in the way a congregation thinks, as well as the manner in which its members live their lives. The past will be left behind. Remembering will help make this transition possible. It is repentance that will serve to restore Christianity and replace churchianity. Repentance is not an option for a congregation. This is because the original word used for repentance is an ongoing command. Repentance is a continuing congregational need, regardless of the age or time of its existence.

- **Prescription # 3** - *"Do"* - Along with remembering and repenting is the third prescription of doing. The church is directed to, "do the first works." It should not be concluded that works are the means required for attaining salvation. Rather, when persons engage in remembering and repenting, the fruit of good works will naturally follow. It is also important to note the language in this three-fold instruction. When Jesus teaches these expectations of remembering, repenting, and doing, His instructions are not optional. In each instance, the words employed are commands. Thus, Jesus expects His church to be willing to consciously and actively incorporate these expectations into their lives. The end of the process will be a renewed spirituality growing out of the Holy Spirits work in the life of the Christian and the church.

Not optional

Reflections

1. What important observation did the author make in the chapter regarding a congregations core values and its attitudes?

2. Can you explain the important role of passion in congregational life?

3. Why do you believe congregations lose passion today?

4. Are you willing to take risks as a Christian? Give a personal example of a risk you have taken.

5. Is your congregation willing to step out and take risks in ministry? Give an example or two if you answered yes to the foregoing question.

6. Why do you think your church is unwilling to take ministry risks?

7. What promises are extended in Scripture to those willing to take great leaps of faith?

8. The author offered his insights on churchianity. Can you explain what he meant?

9. What is the difference between churchianity and Christianity?

10. A scriptural procedure was given for escaping churchianity. Give the scriptural procedure offered by the author.

OFFERING SOME MORE SOLUTIONS

—∿—

"If you are going to have ideas ahead
of the times, you will have to get used to living
with the fact that most people are going
to believe you are in the wrong."
(Bruce Lloyd)

Chapter Five

Incorporating Functional Excellence

Another area of concern with unhealthy congregations relates to the issue of performance. Simply stated, many congregations have settled for operating with mediocrity in place of functioning with excellence.

What is meant by the use of the word excellence? It is a quality revealing a congregation is focused on being the best at whatever it is doing. Continuing to function with established or routine habits indicates a church has chosen to

Excellence is being the best at whatever one is doing.

simply "get by," and to by-pass excellence. Yet, in all organizations today, and especially in churches, operating with
a high level of excellence is both needed and expected. But
this quality is still missing in many congregations.

Perhaps excellence needs to be defined a bit more. The
reader is not to gather the idea excellence is being equated
with perfection. No congregation will ever achieve abso-
lute perfection. Any congregation choosing to function with
excellence, however, will be able to do many things in a
much better fashion than the way they presently do them.

You are probably thinking the author is focused on the
big things a church does each week. But the big things are
really not the primary focus here. The big things still need to
be done with excellence. Yet, the major concern in this book
is with many small things a congregation can do, and do
well, which will serve to vastly improve its ministry.
When these small areas are carefully addressed a congregation's increased effectiveness will become highly visible.
In fact, a congregation's improved performance will save it
from the crisis of stagnation.

Consider, for example, a congregation's baby nursery. If
your church is planning on having young families in atten-

dance, be sure your baby nursery is operating with excellence. This will involve:

- Having a nursery clean, safe, spacious, eye catching, and functional.
- Having a nursery well staffed, along with modern conveniences.
- Having a nursery staffed with knowledgeable, cheerful, sensitive, and caring volunteers.
- Having a nursery with workers who are in the nursery well in advance of starting times at all services and activities.

If you are not ready ahead of time for the arrival of infants, you will have a major strike against your church. For without providing an increasing excellence in this area a younger family will not choose to identify with your church.

How about your restrooms?

- Are they clean?
- Are they bright?
- Are they roomy?
- Are they modern?
- Are they free of offensive odors?

- Do they always have hand soap and toilet tissue in place?

It is a known fact the majority of people today will pay more attention to your nursery and restrooms than they will your sanctuary and classrooms. People increasingly expect a high level of excellence in these small yet often unnoticed areas of your church.

Allow the author to touch on one more small area in congregational life. How does your church choose to have contact with people who visit your services? It is not enough to have a nice building for them to enter. Nor is it enough to have one or two greeters at your entry doors.

You need to have a greeting process in place touching people from the time they arrive in your parking lot until they are inside your building. In fact, three or more personal contacts are crucial for guests who choose to visit your church for the first time. Their return is unlikely if you have not provided an effective greeting system with which to welcome them.

There are also a few more small areas to consider. When they are seriously addressed you can expect some big improvements to take place in your church.

- One important area is beginning your services on time. A church falling into the trap of starting services late creates a bad practice. For one thing, you encourage people to form the habit of coming late to services. You also anger the majority of people who are sensitive about the responsible use of time.

- Another small item, yet one needing improvement in congregations, is in regard to Sunday School teachers arriving ahead of class starting time. A teacher who arrives the moment the class is scheduled to begin, or who comes late, is performing in an irresponsible and damaging fashion. Teachers should be present ahead of time to ready himself or herself, and to prepare the classroom, as well, for the arrival of students. One more serious mistake is for a teacher to fail to secure, in advance, a replacement when he or she is unable to be present to teach on any given Sunday.

- Churches need to be sure there are no gaps in their services. Gaps refer to idle and unoccupied time. It is a serious distraction today, as well as a poor example, for anyone to be slow in getting to the platform for a prayer, or, some other function he or she has been called upon to perform.

- A card ministry is a small ministry with great potential. This ministry can be conducted by one person, a Sunday School class, a leadership team, or even the church ministry staff. It provides a wonderful opportunity for effectively reaching shut-ins, the hospitalized, guests, important events in person's lives, and families at the time of death.

- The appearance of your church building is another matter of great importance to the effectiveness of your congregation. This important, yet, small ministry, involves such areas as, mowing the grass with consistency; keeping the landscape neatly manicured; power washing and tuck pointing an older building; repairing damaged windows and doors; replacing burned out light bulbs; and painting the building whenever and wherever it is needed.

Small things are frequently viewed as being unimportant. But small things develop into big things. Consider pennies as one example. A few pennies do not add up to a huge amount. A jar of pennies, however, equates to a significant sum of money.

The prophet Zechariah raises an important question: "For who has despised the day of small things" (Zechariah 4:10)? Indeed, who can despise small things? It is the small things that add up to the really big things ultimately mattering in life.

Extending Congregational Permission

One major problem faced by congregations today is in the area of freedom. Simply stated, a person is not always free to function or serve in congregational life. Gaining the right to do something in a church, members often discover, can take place only after a considerable degree of red tape and bureaucratic committee action has occurred. By the time permission is granted the ministry need has been forgotten, or, the person wishing to serve has lost his or her zeal for serving.

In conjunction with the thinking pursued here is the often heard cliché, "who gave him or her the right to do what they're doing?" Consider some questions:

- Does every action in a church require a time consuming judicial process before it can be executed?
- Is the foregoing a scriptural expectation?

- Is a red tape process necessary from a rational perspective?
- Will this process foster church health or malignancy?
- Or, is this simply one more way in which congregations have allowed themselves to drift into dysfunctional health?

Bill Easum, who has helped this writer immensely in understanding congregational behavior, makes this important statement, "I am convinced, that making decisions and controlling what happens is more important in established churches than making disciples."[10] Easum is clearly on target. The demon of control is often responsible for destroying Christ's kingdom mission in many congregations.

But why is heavy-handed control practiced? The foregoing question is very important and will require careful attention here. For iron-fisted controllers are heavily engaged today in keeping things under lock and key. These individuals are noted for, "carrying a big stick!"

Furthermore, the problem with iron-fisted controllers has been experienced during the author's time in leadership ministry. It has nonetheless been experienced by other ministers who have told their horror stories of dealing with iron-fisted controllers. Even a number of sensitive church members are aware of controllers and the lethal threat they pose. But again, why is control so often practiced in congregational settings today? Control is practiced for the following reasons:

- They have a personality type lending itself to the exercise of control.

- They rise to a position of power and control because people in churches allow them to do so.

- They sincerely believe a church is meant to be operated in a controlled fashion, which, in all honesty, eliminates the creativity and freedom provided by the Holy Spirit.

- They even struggle with a "messiah complex." Some controllers honestly think God has placed them in authority to keep the house in order.

- They believe a congregation will get off track, and even become an unhealthy fellowship, if some measure of managerial control is not exercised. Yet, they are the only ones who know what to do in these situations. Just ask a controller. He or she will offer you additional descriptive information, when given the opportunity, to further strengthen their position.

The author has discovered controllers emerge in different ways in congregational contexts. Sometimes they develop a controlling attitude as members of a church. The author is thinking of a man and a woman who serve to illustrate this point.

The woman is noted by many persons in her congregation as being the resident "bull dog," or, "general." Church leaders are afraid to make decisions without her blessing. The attempt to understand how she has reached this pinnacle of dominance, and to control, is difficult to comprehend by the uninitiated. But she has nonetheless acquired special sainthood status and clout by many members of her congregation. Furthermore, she assumes the right to be the person who, not only strikes fear in all those who make major congregational decisions, she also assumes the right to instruct new Christians in regard to what they can or cannot do as members of her church.

Allow the author to introduce you to the man's approach with control. He functions more like a security guard. In fact, he even resembles a local small town policeman who carefully watches the traffic flow. His major duty is to keep traffic under control. One example of his security guard mentality comes to mind. He will freely, without authorization to do so, seek to discipline children in the congregation who he believes are acting in improper ways. He has designated himself as the person in charge. And, quite bluntly, he is a master at frightening children and enraging their parents. The man is mean-spirited and displays a very austere and hateful demeanor.

Sometimes, the controllers described will emerge from within the life of a congregation. At other times they will become an appointed church leader seeking to achieve their agenda. They will either jockey for becoming a leader, or, members of a congregation will help propel them into leadership. Controllers are not in a church for the purpose of advancing Christ's mission to make disciples. Rather, they are in place to keep order as they believe it was meant to be kept. In short, they serve as, "keepers of the aquarium."

The mindset to control things is obviously a congregational roadblock today. It is also a frustrating experience for ministry leaders who must put up with the evil that goes on daily, on the part of controllers, in congregational life. For when controllers are at work they make the church an unhealthy context in which to grow and serve. One should never forget the work of controllers is a clever tool of the devil to hinder a congregation from achieving God's mission. He will use this tool effectively to sidetrack a congregation and lead it in wrong directions.

The problem is now clearly out in the open. Yet, how does a church go about overcoming the demon of control? In other words, how can a church go about disarming this devilish practice today?

- The demon of control can be overcome as high visibility is given to the nature of the problem. Frequently, controllers operate in an undetected fashion. As a result, many congregations have accepted their actions as the way church is to be done. This is why the author is providing the material in his book. Until the nature of the problem is laid open, congregations are unable to do anything to alleviate what is causing the trouble.

- The demon of control can be overcome when a congregation consciously becomes a body of Christian believers, and ceases being an institution laden with numerous rules and regulations. This is a crucial area in which change must take place. For

Church should be about Kingdom issues,

the church is not a human organization concerned with enforcing business matters. It is about kingdom issues, and not about what Bill Easum calls, "running the church."[11] Far too many churchmen mistake "running the church" with doing God's will.

- The demon of control can be overcome when serving on a church committee is replaced with serving the Lord according to people's abilities or gifts. Bill *Serve according to giftness* Easum sees committees as one of the problems severely hindering congregations.[12] As a leadership minister, the author has learned firsthand how problematic committees can be to the body of Christ. Committees do an excellent job of stifling congregational action in place of encouraging a congregation to act decisively.

- The demon of control can be overcome when rigid procedural controls in congregations are replaced with being a permission giving church.[13] Congregations need to develop an open attitude of love encouraging church members to serve according to their God given gifts. Yet, until this happens, congregations will continue to be nothing more than bottlenecks. In other words, they will function as courts

Be a Permission giving church,

Serve according to God given gifts

of law in place of being fellowships of love and understanding.

Recovering Ministerial Respect

Another area needing attention is in regard to the way leadership ministers are often treated today. The majority of persons in a congregation view their leadership minister as a special gift to their church. They understand he is present to show their congregation the direction in which it needs to go. In short, they have great respect for their ministerial leader, believing he is called by God to provide spiritual leadership.

Yet, another contingent of persons view the minister differently. They are not intentionally hostile toward him. Nor are they focused on opposing him. They just have a different perspective with regard to the minister's role from the perspective given in the opening paragraph.

Simply stated, they view the minister as a "hired hand." He's the pastoral leader called to do the job traditionally done in their church. They serve as his observers to make sure he does the job in the way they believe it should be done. When he performs as expected, he is applauded. But when he veers from the established path, he is resisted, resented, and generally severely criticized. If enough discontent is engendered against him, an attempt will be set in motion to have him removed from his ministerial duties.

The adversarial group just described is normally most formidable. Furthermore, they are very tenacious, with some of them being very mean-spirited. They are nonetheless talented at amassing support, and they have learned, as well, the effective maneuvers required for having a minister "fired." Yet, removing one of these entrenched controllers is much like trying to remove an elephant out of ones pathway.

Here is another sad item about this adversarial group. They represent but a fraction of a congregation's membership. Yet, they are able to stir enough discontent to effectively achieve their misdirected aim of ridding a congregation of its minister.

Members who love their minister, however, are frequently left wondering what actually happened to bring about his removal. When they finally realize the underhanded tactics used to remove him, they become disillusioned. Sometimes they will leave a church. At other times they will grow half-hearted in their Christian commitment, and will eventually join the group known as, "inactive members," in a congregation.

This picture of the divergent view of the minister's role is painted for an important reason. It is this traditional and misdirected view of the minister just described that is causing much of the current dysfunction in congregational life. Furthermore, it is perpetuating a tradition for lulling the church into a serious non-growth pattern.

Quite honestly, a majority of congregations are on a plateau, or, they are going backwards. They do not realize their church is in its unhealthy condition because of the disrespectful position in which they have placed their pastoral leader.

Ministers are trained and equipped in colleges and seminaries to provide congregational leadership. They are given the necessary tools and skills required for taking hold of the church wheel and propelling it forward in positive ways. But the freedom to lead the ship is, more often than not, removed from ministers in many traditional congregational settings today.

A minister feels like a person who is placed behind the steering wheel of a vehicle. The vehicle is moving forward at break neck speed. But his hands are cuffed, and he cannot free them in order to take hold of the church wheel and direct it in ways he knows are needed.

Numerous congregations are guilty of placing their minister in this helpless role just described. The congregations doing this sincerely believe they are doing the right thing. Yet, their hand tying tactics have placed their church and minister in a pathetic and helpless position. They have designed both for suffocation and death.

Congregations are much like the frog in the kettle George Barna describes in one of his earlier books.[14] Should you place a frog in a pan of boiling water, it will sense the danger and leap to its safety. But if you place a frog in water at room temperature, and gradually increase the heat, the frog will remain in the water until it boils to death.

The same thing happens in many congregations today. They have adapted well to their environment. In fact, their adaptation has been much to perfect. Many congregations are about to boil to death in their own surroundings. Like Barna's frog in the kettle they have become victims of their own environment. Unless a serious mediating effort is undertaken on their behalf these congregations will die.

But how can the frog in the kettle be saved from its dangerous position?

- The rescue can happen when a church is able to see clearly its own plight. The frog does not recognize its dangerous position. Thus, it boils to death. The same thing happens to congregations. The attempt in this book is to help a congregation see its plight before it is to late, and move a church to jump courageously from its boiling pan of water.

- The rescue can happen when our ministers are restored to a position in which they can provide the healthy direction and leadership for a church required and needed. They should be allowed to do the foregoing for two reasons. First of all, God has called them to provide leadership for the church. Secondly, they have been given the skills and tools necessary to effectively lead the church in its mission.

- The rescue can happen when churches go to work in changing the style of leadership endangering congregations and ministers. Persons are not meant to be positioned in congregations to operate as iron-fisted controllers. They are placed in a church to assist in fulfilling the Lord's mission in their community, and in the larger world.

- The rescue can happen when a congregation can see the big picture offered in the table which follows. It attempts to show the difference between a controlling congregations expectations, when contrasted with the ministers Spirit led understanding of his role and calling.

Perception of the Pastoral Leaders Role		
Pastoral Function	**Congregational Leadership Perception**	**Pastoral Leadership Perception**
Leadership	He functions under congregational expectations	He serves as the congregations leader/coach
Preaching	He preaches on topics/themes the congregation and leadership expects	He preaches the Bible as he is led by the Holy Spirit
Visitation	He is expected to visit members	He believes he is to equip members to do home visitation
Evangelism	He is the evangelist	He is to equip members to evangelize
Administration	He oversees/ supervises the church staff within parameters	He oversees/ supervises the church staff

Worship	He leads public worship according to established practice	He designs the public worship experience as he sees the worshipers spiritual needs
Privileges	He possesses some rights	He has the same rights as other members
Duties	The leadership decides his duties	The pastor decides his duties with leadership input
Role Perception	He is a "hired hand" of the congregation and leadership	He is called by God to lead the congregation
Social Role	He has little or no involvement	He decides his social involvements
Communicator	He communicates the wishes of the leadership and congregation	He communicates what he discerns are God's wishes for the congregation, with leadership input
Pastoral Counseling	He counsels with persons as the needs present themselves	He counsels according to the constraints of his ability and time

Ministries	He works within established/ traditional congregational ministries	He helps plan and initiate new ministries to go with existing ministries
Church Attendance	He is responsible for increasing attendance	He is responsible with the leadership and congregation for increasing attendance
Change Agent	He makes changes only as he is permitted to do so	He makes changes freely as he sees the needs

Overcoming Age Barriers

A second area of ministerial abuse is in operation today. Once a minister crosses the fifty-five age mark, a majority of congregations will choose to by-pass him, or dismiss him, as being worthy of serving as a leadership minister. The reasons for by-passing him, or, not considering him, are varied. But here are some of the more prominent ones:

- Older ministers are considered unable to accept and adapt to change. Congregations today must be willing to face and undergo various changes in their approaches to doing ministry. In short, the church is not the same today as it was in the older minister's "hay day" of leadership ministry.

- Older ministers are also thought to be placed in an unfair position when they are called to lead a modern day congregation. The approaches and methods are much different. Thus, he is placed in a position in which he is unprepared, uncomfortable, and out of his realm or domain.

- Older ministers are thought to be unable to be accepted by younger persons in congregations today. They want to be led by a younger minister with whom they can identify, and with whom they can comfortably serve.

- Older ministers, unlike younger ministers, are unwilling to be shaped by the expectations of growing congregations. They believe they need a minister who can grow and develop with them. Congregations do not believe an older minister is able to make the changes required.

- Older ministers also experience having an outright bias against them, by some congregational members, in which they are thought to be disqualified, due to their age. Many congregations do not wish to call or to retain a more mature minister to be their leader. This is not legal by law, nor is it a fair and just practice, yet congregations have chosen to follow this rigid and dogmatic path.

The foregoing criticisms of older ministers are really not justified. While the above reasons for by-passing them might apply to some, they certainly do not apply to all ministers in this age category. In fact, many of these men are more in touch with church ministry today than current churchmen are willing to give them credit. It is unfortunate, however, many congregations, along with their leaders, have judged them as being ineffective and out of touch with the present day demands of ministry.

There are several reasons why this is one of the sad developments emerging in congregational life today:

- Mature ministers possess a wealth of understanding achieved through years of experience in leadership ministry.
- Mature ministers are valuable for having a healthy ministry staff. Furthermore, congregations need a variety of ages represented. Yet, older ministers are

able to provide the competent and able leadership needed for the overall staff.

- Mature ministers are able to serve as strong mentors to younger ministers. They are able to give them valuable direction for the present, and the needed assistance required for the ministry road yet ahead of them. Mature ministers can help younger ministers avoid many of the mistakes and pitfalls they have already made. Even after mistakes have been made, a mature minister can assist a younger minister in living through the traumas they will undergo, and help them move ahead once again in leadership ministry.

There is one final area of ministerial abuse needing to be addressed here. It is in regard to younger ministerial leaders. These men are in the process of ministerial training, or, they are a recent college or seminary graduate. They are novices or beginners in the practice of ministry. They possess the training required for providing leadership, but they have not had the opportunity of actually experiencing hands-on ministry in a local congregation.

Ones early days in leadership ministry can either be encouraging times, or, they can be times in which the young minister becomes discouraged and driven out of leadership ministry. For a beginning ministry can either be a God-send, or, it can be a young mans nightmare. Quite honestly, a beginning ministry can either make or break a young minister who is trying to find his way through the dense wilderness of church life.

The author's youngest son Matt was fortunate to have had a very positive experience when he began church leadership ministry. While a junior at St. Louis Christian College he began serving with a small congregation in Modesto, Illinois. The church freed Matt to complete his college training. Yet, he was invited by the church to serve with them on weekends, and was allowed to miss a Sunday when college expectations demanded that he do so.

During this relatively short ministry with the Modesto church, Matt received a start in church ministry. He had the opportunity of doing the preaching and teaching; engaged in visitation; conducted weddings and funerals; attended various types of meetings; counseled; and was invited into the homes of persons for meals and other kinds of family gatherings. The church loved and cared for Matt in a very special way. Matt loved this church and continues to love them and remembers their example to this day.

Here are a few of the happy and healthy results of this ministry for Matt:

- He developed a passionate love for the people who formed the life of this very special congregation.
- He grew in his ability and skill to communicate the message of Scripture in preaching and teaching.
- He developed a basic understanding of the functions for being a leadership minister in a local congregation.
- He received the affirmation from the church needed for encouraging him to continue in ministry and to do additional seminary training.
- He was encouraged by members who chose to attend many of his college basketball games, as well as his college graduation.

Matt had a great beginning. It would be wonderful if every young man was just as fortunate as Matt. But with Matt's success story, there are horror stories of beginning ministers. Some of these young men have been wounded and scarred for the rest of their lives. Others have chosen to vacate ministry leadership altogether.

What can be done to change this negative picture for those ministers beginning their lives in leadership ministry?

Allow the author to offer a few suggestions:

- Congregations need to see their mistake in practicing iron-fisted or controlling management styles.

- Congregations need to engage in Christianity and not continue in the misdirected practice of churchianity. There is a great difference between the two.

- Furthermore, as leadership ministers are required to train for leading a congregation, congregations need to be trained in regard to how a church is to receive and treat a ministerial leader.

- Finally, abusive congregations could be helped out of their negative condition by observing and learning from those congregations enabling them to see a more positive and Christian way to function.

Reflections

1. Does your congregation function with excellence? Explain.

2. Are you aware of areas in your congregation in which excellence is presently needed?

3. Do you believe respect for a pastoral leader is missing in your church? If so, explain carefully.

4. Is your minister allowed to provide leadership in your congregation? Why, or, why not?

5. Do you believe George Barna's analogy of the frog in the kettle is a good one to use in relationship to the church today?

6. Is your church guilty of forfeiting the right of an older minister to be your pastoral leader? Why?

7. What values would a mature leader be able to bring to your congregation?

8. Congregations believe pastoral leaders should receive college and seminary training. Should our churches be trained on how to receive a pastoral leader? Explain carefully.

9. Are you aware of another solution enabling a malignant church to become a magnificent church?

10. What should be done to protect our pastoral leaders from congregational abuse? What should be done to protect our congregations from pastoral abuse?

HEALTHY CONGREGATIONAL BENCHMARKS

—⟋⟍—

"There are no shortcuts to anyplace worth going."
(Beverly Sills)

Chapter Six

Regarding Church Doctors

When the author had completed the requirements for receiving his Doctor of Ministry Degree, he anxiously awaited its conferral. The words of the academic dean will long be remembered. At the graduation ceremonies he requested the DMin candidates to rise and face the podium.

Before inviting the candidates to come forward and receive their degrees, he put a label on them in the presence of the gathered audience. He referred to the DMin candidates as, "doctors of the church." Wow! This label was shocking.

"Me, a doctor of the church," I chuckled? A minister being tagged a doctor is probably the last thing a congregation wants to hear.

Later, the author was looking at what those receiving the DMin degree were attempting to achieve. He discovered the degree was meant to prepare the candidates to think in a theological and critical fashion regarding the church. Thus, the label placed on the DMin candidates was really not a bad one at all.

Thinking critically is not a popular activity today. Theologians tend to be disregarded by lay persons, as they are viewed as an elite clan of knit pickers. They are viewed as troublesome types, and as those who are unnecessarily negative. Some would choose to align theologians with the ancient clan of legalists in the time of Jesus known as Pharisees.

One major conviction is dominant regarding theologians. It is generally believed they are time wasters. They are viewed in this manner because they engage in scrutinizing a lot of jots and tittles in their academic labs. This meticulous approach has a tendency to drive common folks right out of their minds.

But theologians are still around. They have not left the arena. No one has removed them from the scene. They are still probing the issues they deem important in the study of the roots of Christianity.

And let's face it, without some intelligent theological thinking we would not be able to continue as faithful stewards of the Christian faith. Furthermore, we would have a lot less understanding of Christianity if theologians were absent from the scene. Theologians are doctors in the realm of theological thought, as physicians are doctors of the body.

Is it not also natural to conclude if doctors are necessary in the deeper areas of theology, doctors are also necessary for thinking theologically and critically regarding the church today? For theology is meant to serve the interests and welfare of the church. So, maybe, the academic dean was not on the wrong track when he suggested those receiving the Doctor of Ministry degree were to become, "doctors of the church."

The author's thinking needs to be taken one step further. Without clear thinking in reference to the church, it becomes highly probable church folks will believe in anything and everything as being acceptable in church life. Thus, as doctors of the church, the recipients were not receiving the degree to become passive church leaders and educators. The DMin candidates were being prepared to offer the church a healthy theological framework out of which to responsibly function.

Having "doctors of the church" is not now as crazy as the author once thought it was. For the church will always, regardless of the age, need critical thinkers to keep it biblically alert and functional. God selects and prepares certain individuals to be His church diagnosticians for their age.

Since that time in which the author was first dubbed a "doctor of the church," he has encountered this label being used in other places as well. For example, he has seen the designation used by those who function as church consultants. Their role is one of being a health diagnostician. For congregations, like physical bodies, can become ill, and they will need the help of a church doctor.

When sickness does occur diagnostic procedures are required for helping a congregation overcome its malady. Should healing not be achieved a congregation will continue to ineffectively limp along. Or, should worse occur, a congregation may even experience a point of termination.

In the present day there are some established medical procedures for identifying and treating health related problems. Educators are also available who have developed criteria for determining the academic progress of students. Even coaches have ways of knowing when members of their team are playing at their optimum level.

Considering the Benchmarks

But, what are the observable benchmarks for identifying a healthy church? When church diagnosticians utilize the measuring lens of Scripture, and then observe congregations functioning in scripturally healthy ways, they are able to identify some of the more important benchmarks for lifting congregations out of ill health and into a more stable condition. This being true, the author and readers are now ready to consider some major benchmarks of healthy congregations.

Successful and healthy congregations possess certain notable qualities. These qualities may be labeled as benchmarks. The qualities offered in these pages are the author's benchmarks for having a healthy congregation today.

Note the word benchmark a bit further. This term refers to those qualities which help describe something as being healthy and growing. Additionally, anything labeled a benchmark must meet certain standards, or, a set of measurements.

Congregations have two observable standards available for drawing data to understand the benchmarks of a healthy church. These two sources are the Scriptures, and those congregations that have been noted as being successful in incorporating these scriptural benchmarks into their ministry.

The author earlier pointed out that he had maintained a notebook of clichés mirroring an unhealthy congregation. He has now balanced this earlier cliché notebook with an additional notebook containing the benchmark qualities of a healthy church. These qualities help to clearly identify congregational health and well being.

What are these observable benchmarks of a healthy church? Consider the major benchmarks that serve to make a church body a healthy fellowship in which to belong and serve.

Acquiring Kingdom Thinking

What is the starting point for identifying a healthy church? The foundational starting point is moving in the direction of acting on the basis of kingdom thinking. For the major concern of Jesus in His ministry was in regard to the kingdom of God. He did not appear and preach the church. Rather, Jesus came preaching the "kingdom of God . . . because for this reason," He says, "I have been sent" (Luke 4:43).

When Jesus introduced the kingdom in his preaching and teaching, He was not intending to focus his hearer's attention on geographical turf. Rather, the kingdom, as Jesus portrayed it, referred to God ruling or reigning in the hearts and minds of His people.

There are some individuals, however, who have chosen to veer off in the wrong direction. For they have mistakenly chosen to believe God's rule is what takes place in the church. There is a tendency to believe the church and God's kingdom are the same.

Yet, they are not equal. Equating the two is misdirected as it places too much authority and control in the hands of the institutional church today. The kingdom must be allowed to be free to direct and influence how a church thinks and acts. Without Divine direction, a church is unable to continue in its own strength. It must rely on Divine help and assistance.

Scripture makes the foregoing point crystal clear in a couple of different instances.[15]

This needs to be stated in simpler terms.

- What or who determines the direction your congregation chooses to go today? Is the direction you take decided primarily by the majority vote of your congregation?

- Or, are the decisions made in your congregation those based on kingdom thinking and kingdom values?

In far too many instances kingdom decisions are made primarily at the congregational level. When the foregoing happens the Lord is not given the final word. And a church is unable to function according to kingdom thinking when critical decisions are allowed, or permitted to be made, at the congregational level.

Give the Lord the final word

Consider the words of Jesus to His church: "But seek first the kingdom of God and His righteousness, and all these things shall be added to you" (Matthew 6:33). According to the teaching of Matthew, the church is called to seek God's kingdom and righteousness first. Thus, when the church honors the Lord's expectation believers can expect their needs to be met.

Congregations need to do what Jesus would do

While participating in a Bible study group someone said they liked the WWJD bracelets many were wearing. These letters stand for, "<u>W</u>hat <u>W</u>ould <u>J</u>esus <u>D</u>o?" This person also added it was encouraging to be reminded in every situation encountered, sensitivity is needed regarding what Jesus would do at this moment. The suggestion definitely applies to congregations. They require the constant reminder of always needing to engage in, and be guided by, kingdom thinking.

There is a need to highlight for the reader the working difference between kingdom and institutional thinking. Through the use of the following table, one can clearly see the difference between the two extremes when applied to specific categories of congregational life.

Church Categories	Kingdom Thinking	Institutional Thinking
Structure	Operates under a theocracy	Operates under a democracy
Orientation	A sense of outward mission	A sense of inward survival
Authority	Follows Scripture	Follows organizational documents and procedures

Governance	Led by the Holy Spirit	Led by a church board
Focus	Doing ministry	Having meetings
Function	Develops disciples	Seeks to motivate or manipulate church members
Decisions	Made by prayer	Made by rational approaches
Growth	Seeks disciples	Seeks more members
Leadership	Spiritually chosen and prepared	Politically selected and motivated
Money	Believes God provides	Believes church provides
Lifestyle	Practices love	Practices legalism
Future	Heaven is anticipated	Religious success is anticipated

2ⁿᵈ Benchmark

Clarity of Purpose

1ˢᵗ

The first benchmark quality of a healthy church is to be committed to kingdom thinking. This is where a healthy congregation must begin. Apart from a solid kingdom foundation a church is automatically off in the wrong direction. Disaster lies just ahead.

2 Wd Benchmark

At this point there is a need to move to the second benchmark quality. Healthy congregations will possess a clear sense of direction in their ministry. They will know where they are going. If the direction they are headed is not clear everything else they do will become confusing. A congregation directed and undergirded by God's rule will have a keen sense of the direction it must take.

Perhaps a few direct questions would be helpful to consider:

- What is the purpose of your church?
- Why do you exist?
- Do you have any idea where you are headed?
- Are you clear about the road ahead for your congregation and its ministry?
- Can you give clear and concise answers to these questions?

Good questions to follow

Questions like the foregoing ones will cause pastors and church leaders to scratch their heads in confusion. They will try and offer sensible and sane responses, but the responses given will more often than not, lack clarity.

Furthermore, should you choose to look at a set of congregational by-laws they will often fail to give a clear understanding as to why a church exists. The purpose or purposes given tends to fall in one of two confusing directions:

- Either the stated purpose is much too vague to make sense.

- Or, it will give reasons for a congregation's existence having little or nothing to do with its scriptural calling as a body of believers.

Disciple Making

The reason a church exists relates to its scriptural responsibility in the area of disciple making. Congregations faltering in the area of making disciples fail to understand why they exist. For the ultimate end of being Christ's disciple is to bring glory to God through leading others into Christian discipleship.

Our goal

Disciple making was a ministry of great importance for Jesus. In the Gospels one gathers the significant role this ministry played in His overall game plan for the world. Consider some of the emphases regarding discipleship Jesus gives to His followers in these New Testament documents.

- The major core instruction manual for Christian discipleship is provided by Jesus in the Sermon on the Mount (see Matthew 5-7).

Being disciples

- The disciples of Jesus are to abide constantly in His Word, and to keep His commandments (John 8:31; *And following* 14:15, 23).

- Discipleship is a matter of personal choice. Yet, when one chooses to be a Christian disciple there are great demands and sacrifices to be made (see Matthew 16:24-27).

- Some further expectations are also required of the Christian disciple (see Matthew 10:34-39; Luke 14:25-33).

- God will honor the one who chooses to be His disciple (see John 12:26).

- Jesus commissions His followers to engage in an ongoing lifestyle of making others His disciples (Matthew 28:18-20; Mark 16:15-16; Luke 24:44-49).

3 Steps in Disciple Making → start here

There is also a three-step cycle one is to follow in his or her ministry of disciple making. All three cycles are a crucial part of the overall process. Here is the three-step procedure:

- **Enlistment** - To begin following Christ one needs to be enlisted in His service. Enlistment takes place when a person hears and then heeds the call of Jesus to follow Him. During His earthly ministry Jesus engaged constantly in calling persons to Himself. This ministry continues today as the gospel is faithfully proclaimed and taught by the church. It is a call to Christian conversion and to the kingdom lifestyle.

- **Education** - It is important disciples are called and heed the call extended to them. Once they have responded to the call there is the need to continue learning and growing. This is an educational or learning process. Enlistment is the infant stage. Education is the growth stage in which one is moved beyond childhood into adulthood.

- **Equipping** - The process of discipleship does not end with enlistment and education. A Christian disciple enters the stage of enlisting and educating others. This part of the discipling process is known as, equipping. Once one has been personally enlisted and educated to follow Jesus, he or she will then enter the third cycle of equipping others to do the same. The equipping process needs to be recycled over and over again in congregational life today by Christ's followers.

3rd Benchmark

Regaining Ministry Sensitivity

A most important benchmark quality for a healthy church is in regard to doing ministry. Healthy congregations possess strong ministry sensitivity. In fact, doing ministry is what congregational life is all about. Healthy congregations refuse to merely engage in maintaining the institutional church. Maintenance, or evolving into an established religious club, is not their aim, nor do they want to allow this tragedy to happen.

They wish to honor God by serving Him and others. This perspective on ministry suggests being a follower of Christ is not to be aligned with a religious organization. To the contrary, being a Christian and functioning as a church is to be focused upon serving God and others.

Is the approach to ministry being stressed here, however, something this author has invented? If so, its practice lacks authority. But, ministry is not a function for the church advanced by the author. Ministry sensitivity grows out of specific scriptural understandings.

- Ministry finds its foundation or basis in the ministry of Jesus. He did not emerge on the stage of history with the intention of serving a religious institution.

Ministry grows out of specific scriptural understandings.

151

Instead, He [Jesus] came to earth with the focused purpose of serving God and humankind (Matthew 20:28 and Mark 10:45).

- Ministry is not intended to be exercised only by Jesus. It is also to be practiced by His church. The Letter to the Ephesians points out apostles, prophets, evangelists, and pastors and teachers, were given by the Lord as special gifts to the church (see Ephesians 4:11). As gifts, the roles of evangelists and pastors and teachers is to "equip," or, "enable," the church to minister (see Ephesians 4:12). The purpose of the church is not to become subservient to the expectations of a religious institution.

- Ministry finds its expression in numerous New Testament passages that stress the practice of ministry in relationship to the Christian life. Paul, for example, calls for service from Christians following the connection of their lives to Christ Jesus (see Romans 12:1 and 11).

Thus, ministry is not the idea of the author. Ministry finds its beginning point in New Testament teaching.

Engagement in ministry by God's people is not what is generally seen in established churches today. Rather, traditionally oriented congregations view ministry as emerging within the institutional church, and performed by a select group of persons.

Those in traditional congregations believe that leadership exists for the purpose of serving them. They believe the leadership of the church is to focus major attention on the membership, and especially on the more established members of the church. In short, they believe church leaders are to perform ministry, while church members are positioned to observe and rate their performance.

This is a serious error needing to be addressed and corrected. What are the results of this wrongly perceived practice of ministry in congregational life?

- It serves to prevent the church from modeling its life after New Testament teaching.
- It keeps the church from maturing and having responsible members in God's family. Non-ministering congregations are unhealthy fellowships.
- It is the reason numerous congregations today are unable to grow and are on a plateau, or, they are declining.

But how does a congregation make the transition from receiving ministry to doing ministry? This question needs to be adequately addressed if a congregation is going to make effective progress toward health and magnificence. This transition can take place when congregations intentionally move toward de-centralization.

De-centralization occurs when a congregation is able to move from being a governed church to being a ministering church. A church is governed when a centralized church board is allowed to make major ministry decisions, and to perform the greater portion of a congregation's ministry. Until this structure is changed a congregation will remain an unhealthy fellowship. In fact, a congregation will become composed of idlers, in place of developing into a serving congregation.

When members of a church are engaged in ministry the healthier and more vigorous the congregation will become. Yet, how does this transition occur? By way of the following steps:

- Ministry must be understood and intentionally entered into by the congregation's leadership.
- Members of a congregation must be led to identify their place or places of service by recognizing

their abilities and areas of interest, and then serving according to these strengths.

- Ministry efforts must be encouraged and allowed to openly emerge from within the life of the congregation.

- Ministry teams need to be formed and set free to serve. They will need guidelines and counseling to help them get started, along with a budget to know what monetary resources are available. But they will need freedom to function creatively and responsibly.

- Church leaders need to suggest urgent areas of ministry and encourage believers with accompanying gifts to emerge and meet those needs within the congregation.

- Most importantly, church leaders need to assist ministry teams by way of equipping them; praying with them; encouraging them; providing counsel for them; and not micro-managing them.

Allow the author to provide one example of de-centralization. During one month on the church calendar he was overwhelmed with a huge load of responsibilities. Two sermons were being preached on Sunday morning; a weekly newspaper article was being written; various lessons were being taught; speaking engagements were being fulfilled; and pastoral duties were being conducted in the church.

During this busy time he realized a week of radio devotions was in need of being prepared. Yet, he was unable to identify available time on his schedule to prepare and present these devotions. While praying about the matter the author was led to secure five members from the congregation who would take responsibility for doing a devotional each day of the week. By delegating ministry to other believer's two important ends were achieved. For one thing, he experienced a lightened load. But the better end achieved was the recognition that others had become involved in ministry.

Making a de-centralized move is an important step toward regaining ministry sensitivity in the life of the church. This practice needs to be repeated over and over in congregational life today. It is a benchmark quality necessary for developing a vigorous church that is both healthy and magnificent.

Encouraging Healthy Relationships

Individuals require relationships. They are not optional. God places persons in the world to live together and provide for one another. The attempt to become an isolated person is misdirected, as it will become a serious health hazard to everyone.

Relationships are also needed among God's people. Wholesome relationships serve as one of the important benchmark qualities of a healthy church. Relationships are crucial because being a Christian is not an individual matter. To be a healthy and growing believer, as well as part of a healthy and growing church, will require that every Christian be in the company of other Christians. This need for relationships can be seen in a variety of scriptural contexts.

- God is portrayed in Scripture as being a Trinity, or, . Godhead. The members of the Trinity or Godhead are referred to as the Father, Son and Holy Spirit, but they portray God as a plurality (see Matthew 28:18-20).

- During his earthly ministry Jesus had his "inner circle" of relationships. Though He is frequently pictured alone, Jesus is also seen in the company of a chosen threesome, Peter, James, and John (see Matthew 17:1; and Mark 9:2).

- In forming His Apostolic band Jesus demonstrated the value of relationships. Twelve men were selected

Ultimately strength comes from God - but He meets many of our needs through teamwork w/others.

We all need to be strengthened & encouraged.

esp

to serve as His mission representatives (see Mark 6:7-13). They went out to serve others two by two (see Mark 6:7).

- Consider the church in regard to relationships. The church is an assembly, or, a plurality of individuals formed into a network of responsible members, who function on behalf of one another (see Acts 2:41-47).

Relationships also have an important function for a Christian living a healthy and balanced life. Balance is an issue discussed earlier in this book. When relationships are joined with the other important aspects of Christianity, one possesses the needed balance for developing a healthy life in Christ.

There is a need for the foregoing, as individuals will connect with others for the sake of simply relating. Or, they will become involved in specific relationships to be part of a clique. Church relationships will even be entered into for other advancements being pursued in life.

Yet, there are genuine reasons for relationships that go beyond the superficial motives just given. One important reason for having relationships in the church relates to the

Relationships are needed for encouragement.

need for encouragement. It is not an easy task to live in the world. And it is not an easy task to live in the world as a Christian. When one chooses to incorporate Christ's principles into his or her life there is going to be animosity exhibited. Thus, a Christian needs the support of other believers experiencing the same problems.

The Letter to the Hebrews teaches that Christians are to, "exhort (encourage) one another daily" (Hebrews 3:13). This need for encouragement is taught in Scripture because discouragement was also a problem in Bible times. Without the presence of genuine Christian relationships a believer, like the early Christians, is in danger today of exiting the faith and returning to his or her former way of life. But through healthy Christian relationships courage is infused into the believer and becomes a means of making it possible to continue in the Christian walk.

Relationships are also necessary because persons have a pressing need to belong today. Individuals live in an expanding world. But many still live in their private shells. This is not always done by choice. The kind of world we live in cuts people off from one another. As a result, it is very difficult to form genuine friendships, while at the same time

W/O Christian Relationships, a believer runs the risk of exiting the faith. Healthy Christian relationships infuse courage.

living a responsible life in the world, and caring adequately for one's family.

This was made clear to the author in a visit with a young family who had attended Sunday worship services. Some important things were shared regarding the church. Once the presentation was made an opportunity was given for the couple to ask questions. Their greatest concern was with having individuals in the church with whom they could relate. While they were interested in the church and what was taught, they also needed a context for relationships with persons sharing their Christian values.

Effective evangelism in today's congregations is also very closely attached to healthy group relationships. This was witnessed first hand through a small group in which the author participated. The group was healthy in terms of its internal fellowship. It had structured Bible study and prayer into its life most effectively. Yet, the best part of life in the small group was seeing three of its members become Christians.

A serious problem has been noted, however, with small groups in regard to evangelism. There is a tendency to become in-grown, or, to revert into a private network. In this way they choose to insulate their group. They are reluctant to allow their members to depart from, or, to escape their cozy fellowship. Furthermore, outsiders are prevented from crashing their happy gathering.

Small groups which prevent new persons from joining them create two problems. For one thing, they make their group extremely unhealthy. The foregoing happens when the group forms a fox hole for those with whom they have become comfortable. Yet, a second problem emerges in regard to evangelism. When a group becomes closed it fails to incorporate outreach into its ministry. The church is not intended to be an organization unto itself. Rather, it exists to impact and influence the world. Small groups need to keep this in mind.

It is also true that members are spiritually cared for through the presence of relational connections in church life. Growing congregations require the ongoing spiritual care of their members. When a congregation fails to address the needs of its people it will lose these individuals. And as McIntosh and Martin suggest, you need to find them and keep them.[16]

There was a time in which pastoral care was practiced by a pastoral minister. One person largely did it all. This was expected by the church. No longer is it possible, however, for a single person to accomplish this ministry. When this happens, congregations are turned into maintenance organizations. To expand and grow pastoral care must be incorporated into the small group settings of a congregation.

Pastoral ministers today need to understand the foregoing lesson if they want to see their congregation grow. No longer can they be the lone pastor. A healthy church will need to have pastoral care practiced within its small groups to be able to reach a larger number of people. Yet, many pastors have chosen the path of feeding their egos on being a caring and loving shepherd. Personal ego must be sacrificed if a church is going to move out of its maintenance mode, and become a growing organism.

This has been a difficult transition for the author. Serving as a pastor, as he has been taught, is to give hands on care to the larger membership. But this is really a flawed understanding. One pastor can no longer give individual attention to the entire membership of a church, especially a larger congregation. Furthermore, it does not enable the church to engage in the ministry of pastoral care with their pastor. When he moves on or dies, he can no longer meet those needs like he has done in the past. But the presence of well equipped small groups in pastoral care can enable the church to carry on this important ministry.

One more crucial issue needs to be addressed in reference to relationships and small groups. This issue has to do with small groups being effectively equipped. It is the author's conviction that small groups need to be well prepared to understand their purpose or reason for existence. A group is not formed as an end unto itself. Unhealthy congregations will continue to be unhealthy when they allow small groups to move in wrong directions. Here are a few important features of a healthy small group:

- The group needs a facilitator. This means the group will need someone to provide both structure and direction for the group's activities. Without a facilitator chaos will reign.

- The group will also need a host. In other words, a person, or, family, will provide the place where the small group meets. Some groups will allow each participant to host a meeting.

- The group will need a time for open sharing. There will need to be an opportunity for visiting informally. Perhaps a light meal, or light refreshments, could be provided during this time. Yet, informal time should not be allowed to dominate the group meeting.

- The group will need to spend time in Scripture study and prayer. The study should be on something specific, with the group facilitator guiding the study. While some basic information and instruction is necessary from the facilitator, the study is not to become his or her formal lecture time. Opportunity should be provided for group members to ask questions and make comments. No participant should be allowed, however, to dominate the study through excessive talking. Along with Bible study is the additional need for prayer time. The group should be praying for specific needs and concerns within their group. Items of praise should also be included in the prayer time.

- Group members will need to be sure they have, as one of their goals, to bring two or three unchurched persons into their group. If a small group remains closed and static, evangelistic growth will be downplayed and discouraged.

- The group will need to be aware of the abilities and interests present among them. New ministries within a congregation can be initiated when persons emerge within a small group giving evidence of their special giftedness for beginning a new ministry. A group facilitator needs to be alert to such persons, and to capitalize on the opportunity of utilizing these persons within the larger body of Christ.

Finally, a small group needs to be viewed as but one member of the larger body. Every member in the human body is important. You cannot eliminate any of the body's members. For each member contributes toward the well being of the whole body. The same holds true for the church. When small groups are functioning in a healthy manner they will contribute toward the health and well being of the larger church. When they are not functioning in the proper manner the larger church body will suffer. The church will fall into disunity and chaos. Be sure your small group contributes toward making your congregation a healthy church body.

Reflections

1.   The author uses the word benchmarks in this chapter. What does the author mean by the use of this term?

2.   Two standards were given for understanding the desirable benchmarks of a healthy church. Give these two standards.

3.   How does kingdom thinking differ from institutional thinking?

4.   According to the author, what is the scriptural purpose of a congregation?

5.   Can you state the author's three-step cycle in disciple making? Explain each of the cycles.

6.   What is wrong with a church expecting to be served in place of serving?

7.   How is a church able to make the move out of being served to becoming a serving church?

8. Are relationships important and healthy in the life of a congregation? Explain.

9. Is it possible for relationships in congregations to become unhealthy? Give your thoughts.

10. The church is labeled a body in Scripture. Do congregations require health checkups?

More Healthy Congregational Benchmarks

—ᴍ—

"To lead a symphony, you must occasionally turn
your back on the crowd."
(John Olds)

"Be willing to change. And when you've changed,
be willing to change again."
(This is God, according to Phil Vassor)[17]

Chapter Seven

Moving Toward Restoration[18]

The author is part of the church tradition known today as the Restoration Movement. Emerging on American soil around the year 1800, the movement's early pioneers were focused on returning to the Scriptures as their only authoritative manual for faith and practice. Rejecting creedal statements, they made the Scriptures their final source of authority. A major slogan states the movement's position best: "Where the Bible speaks we speak, and where the Bible is silent we are silent."

It should be stressed here that the Restoration Movement was an outgrowth of the Reformation Movement. Those within the Restoration Movement were largely influenced by the earlier efforts of the Reformers who preceded them. Yet, they believed simply reforming the church was not enough. For the Reformation Movement was unable to achieve the ultimate end needed. Only a radical return to New Testament roots, in the view of these early pioneers, was capable of bringing the church back to its original state and purpose.

The foregoing approach is clearly understandable. For dysfunction cannot be corrected or repaired by the mere band-aid act of reforming something. This only serves as a temporary healing. It would not solve the underlying problem. Much more was required. Specifically, congregations needed to be restored to their original state if they were going to be able to function responsibly in the present day.

But the movement toward restoration is needed for another important reason. Churches are constantly impacted by the twin evils of time and culture. Both of these evils serve to take congregations out of sync and move them in wrong directions. When this happens only restoration can serve to enable congregations to get their bearings and return to their original teaching and way of life.

This was well illustrated by a restoration leader of past days named Carl Ketcherside. Carl gave an analogy with the Mississippi River that helps to establish the issue regarding time and culture and its intrusion upon the church. He says: "In St. Louis the drinking water is taken from the Mississippi River. At its inception this stream is clear and cool. Its waters are pure and invigorating. But on its rolling advance through the states it picks up filth and sediment until by the time it reaches our city it is a chocolate colored body laden with foreign matter. Huge pumps take the water from the channel and direct it into filtration plants. Here it is restored to its original purity."[19]

The Restoration Movement seeks to do something similar in the life of the church today. It serves as a much needed filtration process enabling the church to have restored something of its original purity. Congregations can never be perfect, or without flaw, but they can reclaim a measure of their original impetus and influence.

One misleading idea of restoration needs to be removed. There are some who believe the effort to restore the church is one of bringing back into play a host of first century cultural practices. But that is not the case. Instead, restoration is an attempt to restore, or to put back into practice, those major spiritual principles having made the church a vessel of Divine impact in history.

The New Testament needs to be read and studied in its entirety to gather what constitutes the essential principles of a restored church. But the second chapter of Acts is a key chapter for understanding the bare and basic principles of church restoration. When these principles are restored to their functional position one will be able to experience a malignant church being transformed into a magnificent church. Briefly note some of the essential features engendering restoration in the present time.

- The power of the Holy Spirit will be present and in operation, as was true of the first century church (note Acts 2:1-13).

- The church will focus on preaching and teaching Christ to its generation, and it will not bend to the intrusion of foreign or cultural subject matter. The chief focus in preaching Christ will direct the hearer's attention to His miracles, His death, His resurrection, and His being exalted as both

Lord and Christ. This was, in essence, the nature of Peter's preaching (Acts 2:14-36).

- The preaching will powerfully lead persons to yield their lives to Christ as it happened on the Day of Pentecost. (Acts 2:37-41).

- The church will continue to engage in the teaching of the apostles, to fellowship together, to partake of the Lord's Supper, and to pray as a unified body (Acts 2:42).

- The church will experience miraculous things happening among them; live their lives in humility and unity; share the material things they possess with one another; participate in shared meals and responsible communal life; they will be a happy group and will constantly engage in praising God; and the church, as a result, will add to their growing number of believers daily (see Acts 2:43-47).

One of the great achievements of the Restoration Movement heritage was the slogans handed down for future generations. The most important slogan was the following one: "In essentials, unity; in non-essentials, liberty; in all things, love. The Restoration Movement attempted to make a clear distinction between what was and what was not essential. It is unfortunate, however, that many churches in our day have made necessary what is not really essential. Consider some examples:

- A public service of worship can only be conducted in one way. Multiple approaches to conducting worship services are unacceptable.

- The music utilized in corporate worship can only be one kind of music. A new or different style of music is blasphemy or heresy.

- All decisions in a church must be approved by the congregation through a democratic process. Without congregational approval nothing has the right to exist.

- A church service can only be conducted once, and it must be conducted at the same time every Sunday.

- Everyone in a church needs to be kept happy, or, the congregational leadership is not doing its job.

- It is necessary in a church for everyone to see every-thing just alike.

- Preachers and church leaders must wear a suit and tie at church services.

- Women have no right to be up front leading in public worship over men.

Are any of the foregoing items really essentials in Scripture? If one is honest he or she would be compelled to say not a one of them are essential or binding upon Christians today. Yet, congregations have allowed themselves to fall into the trap of making these items mandatory. Why do congregations tend toward sidetracking into the realm of non-essentials?

- One reason is that traditions emerge resulting in being placed on the same level with, or, actually come to replace, Scripture. These traditions are forced upon church members in both written and unwritten forms today.
- A second reason is over time rational eyes become blurred. Persons lose sensitivity for what matters. They replace the essential things with non-essential things.
- And lastly, God given liberty is replaced with wrongly established convictions. Convictions are used to pound people into established camps, and the supreme virtue of love is lost. One should not forget

the final part of the Restoration Movement slogan, "in all things, love."

The dangerous aspect associated with majoring in the non-essentials is that congregations become unhealthy. In fact, a church majoring in the non-essentials becomes a church dangerously malignant. The presence of this malignant cancer will eventually render a church ineffective, or, bring about its death. On the other hand, healthy congregations are able to make a notable distinction between what is and what is not essential. But what are the main essentials for a congregation to maintain? Allow the author to be suggestive here rather than exhaustive.

- The first major essential is the authority of Scripture. It is the congregations foundational manual for faith and practice. All other documents are not equal with the authoritative position of the Word of God.

- Secondly, belief in the Trinity or the Godhead (see Romans 1:20; and Colossians 2:9). This is an acceptance and belief in the Father, Son, and Holy Spirit. Though separate in function and purpose, they are one, as each is God revealing Himself to humanity in different ways.

- Thirdly, belief in God's justifying and redemptive plan for saving sinful humanity (see Ephesians 2:8-10). Divine action is required to make salvation possible, and for its corresponding human appropriation by faith (Romans 1:16-17).

- Fourthly, the church is God's provision for evangelizing the world; educating Christians; and equipping believers for Christian service (see Matthew 28:18-20; Mark 13:10; and Ephesians 4:11-16).

- Fifthly, the expectation of Christ's return or second coming is an essential belief for Christians (see Matthew 24:30-31; Luke 21:27-28; Mark 13:26-27; and John 14:1-6).

- Sixthly, the reception of heaven will be the ultimate reward for Christians who have persevered to the end of time on earth (see John 14:1ff; and Philippians 3:20-21).

- Lastly, the recognition of punishment in hell will be reserved for those who have not received Christ as Savior and Lord (see II Thessalonians 1:7-10).

Seeking Over Stealing[20]

Scripture also focuses on the need for congregations to seek the lost (see Luke 19:10). Seeking the lost and making disciples is what congregational life is all about. Aside from this focus a congregation lacks clear direction. The sad result of the failure to make disciples means the lost will remain outside of God's fold of safety. The lost are those who are without the saving knowledge of Christ Jesus in their lives. And these persons form the nucleus of helpless sheep who should not be allowed to remain distant from the loving provisions of life with God inside the sheepfold.

Yet, it is amazing many congregations today are suffering from a serious form of amnesia. They are not concerned with reaching the lost. Rather, they are concerned with stealing members from other churches. It is not uncommon these days to hear of congregations increasing in size. But much of their growth is transfer growth.

What is meant by transfer growth? This kind of growth means congregations are guilty of playing the game of exchanging members from one church to another. Church leaders believe transfer growth is church growth in action. Church members, on the other hand, view it as shopping for the right church with which to belong. Yet, this kind of growth does not represent, nor will it accomplish, the kingdom growth taught in the New Testament. It will not enable the church to seriously penetrate the ever-growing darkness of the times, and to make a lasting difference in person's lives through the power of the gospel message.

It is the author's conviction that congregational sheep stealing makes way for an increased dose of unhealthy congregational life. It is unhealthy because it is not a biblical practice. On the other hand, healthy congregations are engaged in seeking the lost in place of stealing sheep. Congregations stealing sheep from other churches become unhealthy fellowships. They are unhealthy for some obvious reasons:

- They are not functioning in the manner taught in the New Testament. In short, they are not seeking the lost with whom Christ Jesus was concerned.
- They are developing a clubhouse mentality in place of a genuine fellowship.
- They are bringing members into their congregation with a confusing array of cultural and religious baggage that will eventually erupt into a divisive context.
- They are not training members to think correctly about what it means to be the church.

- And finally, they are focused on pleasing and winning the admiration of people in place of pleasing God.

Congregations making a lasting difference in these troubled times are those congregations possessing a New Testament sensitivity and orientation to their life and witness. They are focusing on seeking the lost around them, and not on stealing members from other congregations. In other words, they are focusing on converting persons in place of simply gaining, or, growing a membership club.

It is not intended for congregations to be in competition with one another. The enemy is not neighboring churches. Rather, the devil is the enemy needing to be kept in view. He is working a very subtle game plan today to set congregations against one another. His game plan is to encourage focusing on who can accumulate, or soak up, the largest number of church members. If a church is able to control a greater number of members, a church is thought to be growing and prospering. These congregations are even held up before the eyes of others as visible models to follow today.

Recently, while visiting with a pastor in another state the author was shocked with his story. He explained what a church in his area was seeking to accomplish. Like a sponge, this congregation was soaking up the members of other churches into their web. The tactics used to reach these persons, however, was the most disturbing part of all. Consider some of the approaches being used as described by this pastor.

- They were seeking to reach members of area congregations in place of seeking the unchurched, or, the lost around them.

- They were seeking to target and draw members from area congregations they knew were going through times of trouble and unrest.

- They programmed appealing activities that bordered on being theatric, novel, and more entertaining than they were spiritual.

- They advertised in ways that were clearly efforts to put down area congregations, and show how they were a refreshing alternative to the stale and lifeless churches around them.

- They circulated CD'S and DVD'S of their programs and activities through their members, who had influence over members in other churches.

- They were making targeted appeals to reach young families through more sophisticated and novel ways of attracting their children. The church understood parents respond more to their children's wishes and wants, than they do to what is needed in the spiritual development of their children.

Congregations seeking to grow through the foregoing means are unhealthy fellowships. They cannot be described as healthy, even though numerical growth is occurring. These congregations are ill because they function in non-biblical ways. They attempt to reach church members who only help to further develop the ever-growing ill health taking place in congregational life today.

The direction of the ministry of Jesus was one of seeking the lost. Luke establishes the foregoing point in the fifteenth chapter of his Gospel, as he gives the parables of the lost sheep and the lost coin. The emphasis in these parables is on seeking the lost, not on those who have already been found.

How do churches overcome the problem presented here? This is the important question for consideration. A step in the right direction in overcoming this congregational disease of stealing members is when churches are sensitized to the following recognitions:

- When they understand the heart of God for the lost.

- When they realize the terrible future consequences for those who remain among the lost.
- When they experience the joys associated with finding the lost.
- When they view the healing taking place in marriages and families when the lost are reached and reclaimed.
- When they encounter the positive blessings taking place through the numerous lives having been changed and transformed.
- When they see those lives once hostile to Christ and to the church become healthy and holy lives within our churches and communities.

There are a host of newer congregations today that are biblical in the way they function. Instead of growing through transfer growth they are congregations existing for the unchurched. These congregations will even discourage persons transferring from other congregations, as they will be uncomfortable in a church where seeking the lost, and not simply having church members, becomes the primary object of concern.

These congregations are the ones to take note of and to learn from in the present time. For they represent a growth that is both biblical and healthy. Furthermore, they help keep congregations on a firm footing, in place of dipping off into a cultural churchianity which turns people away from institutional churches.

Preaching Connective Sermons

One more benchmark quality of a healthy church is offering sermons that connect.[21] This benchmark suggests a sermon will possess certain qualities to make it an inviting experience for the hearers.

Connective sermons will possess a two-edged sword. The one side of this sword recognizes a sermon must be scripturally based. For a sermon without a scriptural foundation is a sermon lacking God's authority.

The reverse edge of the sword is equally important. A sermon not only needs to be scripturally connected, it also needs to be connected to the hearer's lives. While this side of the two-edged sword is indispensable, Scripture must be the first ingredient to undergird it. Sermons deeply based in Scripture, yet lacking the necessary connective elements for the hearers, runs the risk of becoming a dry and boring lecture. And a religious lecture will not reach, nor will it impact person's lives in today's world.

A growing number of individuals are beginning to downplay the importance of the sermon. These negative voices are suggesting the sermon is no longer accepted and needed as it once was in congregational life. Other types of communication are now thought to be required to replace the sermon.

This viewpoint is most discouraging and unacceptable. For God has chosen preaching as His means of communicating with persons. Present day individuals do not have the right to remove preaching from its God given position.

The author is not convinced preaching has lost its value and place in congregational life. He still believes God works mightily through the preaching of the Word. The ineffectiveness of preaching in our time is due to its loss of connection. In other words, it is in danger of being overly tied to Scripture and neglecting its hearers; or, of being tied to its hearers, yet neglecting its foundation in Scripture. Connective preaching is not an either/or, it is a both/and.

Thom Rainer has written an important text for the church to consider on this matter of the sermon.[22] Those who would choose to downplay the role of preaching need to pay special attention to the material Rainer provides in the introduction to his book. He, along with his research team, discovered that the one major reason why unchurched persons chose to return and visit a church, related to the preacher and his sermon. In fact, this reason was at the top of Rainer's chart. Ninety percent of those who returned to a church did so because of the preacher and the quality of his sermon.

With the foregoing thoughts in mind the author would like to utilize a statement from Michael Fabarez. He says, "Every preacher must be fully assured that his calling to preach is essential to the health of the church, and is unmitigated by modern culture or trends in society".[23]

There are two items in Fabarez's statement needing to be carefully noted. First of all, the preacher must be convinced his preaching is necessary to the health of the church. And secondly, culture and its trends should not be allowed to be the cause of the preacher easing up on his conviction about the place and importance of Christian preaching. Fabarez is clearly on target.

Yet, in order to connect effectively with ones hearers today some important items need to be present in the preachers preaching. High visibility to a few of these crucial areas should be noted to help pave the way toward having connective preaching:

- Initially, a preacher needs to work toward developing a style in which the hearer's interest is maintained. This will involve the use of illustrations, analogies, current events, humor, and anything helping to communicate the meaning of biblical truth.

- Secondly, a preacher needs to present a message having a positive and not a negative character to it. He needs to follow the spirit of Paul's teaching when he said Christians are to speak the truth in love (Ephesians 4:15).

- Thirdly, a preacher needs to learn to use electronic tools in his preaching. He needs to familiarize himself with the use of visual technology. Persons live in a generation impacted more by what they see than by what they hear.

- Fourthly, a preacher needs to understand some practical items in relationship to preaching connective sermons. One item relates to people's attention span. If a sermon is unusually long a preacher is in danger of losing his audience. Maintaining an understandable vocabulary in preaching is also crucial if a preacher is going to connect well with modern day audiences. Connective preaching will also speak in the present tense, and not in the past tense. Perhaps the word K.I.S.S. says it all best - Keep It Short Stupid, and Keep It Simple Stupid.

- Fifthly, a preacher needs to avoid excessive amounts of Scripture quoting. Too much Scripture quoted in a sermon serves to confuse and lull modern audiences to sleep. Scripture is to be used in sermons, but a preacher should not allow a sermon to become a "Scripture quoting" performance. This will cause the preacher to lose the functional connection he wishes to have with his audience.

Developing Healthy Members

The necessary benchmark's for having a healthy church is the consideration in this chapter. And much of the ill health now being experienced is with what congregations have become. Churches have not developed into healthy organizations in which Christians may develop and grow in Christ. Instead, they are plagued by churchianity with the apparent absence of Christianity.

There is a need to refocus attention in the church on the process involved in developing healthy Christians who will become responsible and functioning members in congregational life.

Allow the author to paint a brief picture of what happens in churches today. A person unites with a congregation, and is welcomed as a new member. While he or she attends the services and activities offered, it is not always clear what church membership involves. Church membership often means nothing more than involvement in a lot of meaningless religious routine. As long as a member faithfully attends and supports a church with money, he or she is an accepted and respected member. Furthermore, one is expected to adhere to a variety of congregational procedures, and to participate in the activities offered in its program.

Yet, can one really be a healthy member of a church with these types of expectations? If not, being a church member is more like membership in a club. It is involvement in a business or civic organization, which serves only to occupy ones time and energy. The spiritual meaning of church life is lost in the midst of an institutional emphasis, which only serves to accelerate into additional confusion for its members.

Sensitive church leaders and church members today are asking a lot of searching questions. The following questions are generally the ones heard in congregational life:

- Why am I a member of this church? Why are others a member of this church?

- Why are so few persons in my church actively serving in its life? Why are they merely occupying a pew?

- Why are there a growing number of members labeled inactive members?

- Why does the church frequently lose its members? Some to other churches, and others who leave church life altogether.

- Why is there little excitement along with a sense of growing boredom in congregational life?

How does one answer these questions being asked of churches in our time? The serious questions can be answered by following the thinking being pursued in this book. For the effort here has been to unveil some of the key benchmarks serving to restore the church to magnificence, in place of being a church of dangerous malignancy. The author wishes to focus on those items enabling a church to remain healthy, or, to regain health today. Before looking at those items which promote a healthy church, perhaps there needs to be a brief view of some of the major aspects of an unhealthy church:

- One obvious aspect of an unhealthy church is the actual state of the church itself. Christians cannot grow in a healthy manner in an unhealthy church. Poor health serves to create additional bad health. In short, new members become victims of falling into the same destructive ruts of the troubled and unhealthy church.

- Another aspect of an unhealthy church is the countless number of meetings conducted that members are expected to attend. Churches are more concerned with meetings, or conducting church business, than they are in doing ministry. Congregational leadership seems to possess a penchant for having incessant meetings to talk about problems in place of ministering in their communities. Church leaders, for example, will not miss one of these required meetings. But they are passive in regard to engaging in ministry and kingdom work.

- Outreach is another serious problem in unhealthy churches. For they fail to reach beyond their meeting place. They are more focused on themselves, and have little interest in their community and world. As someone has well said, "the congregation failing to reach out will pass out." Congregations today are clearly in this danger. They have become unhealthy because they have developed passive church members.

- Another problem in unhealthy churches is the controlling members emerging within them. These individuals are mean-spirited and destructively critical. They create a controlling aura in many congregations and keep a church paralyzed. Spreading their evil contagion, controllers give an infectious virus. Controllers are masters at raising others of their own kind. Members who fail to join them will predictably be compelled at some point to leave a church.

- A final problem unhealthy churches encounter is with church hopping on the part of its members. When these persons desire new turf they will begin to check out other church terrains. Once they begin to focus on new church turf, they will very likely begin making excuses. A major line voiced by church hoppers is, "I'm not being fed." It appears these members view the church as an organization existing for entertainment. If it is entertaining them the church is okay. But if it is not providing the entertainment desired, it is time to hop on to another church.

It is now time to look at the positive side of church health. Focusing on the problems without attention to solutions only serves to perpetuate the existing problems. What are some important directions in which the church should go in order to maintain its health? Allow the author to offer some assistance for turning an unhealthy church around to become a healthy church:

- One important step needing to be taken is to rescue the church from its institutional incarceration. The church needs kingdom thinking people and not those who are tied to the institutional church. For when the church evolves into an institution it becomes a monument for admiration, yet ceases being a movement of God impacting people's lives.

- Another important step will involve recognizing the two greatest commandments given by Jesus. These commands enable the church to live according to its nature. The church exists for the purpose of loving God and neighbor (Matthew 22:37-40). Being the church is not about maintaining the institutional church. It is about worshiping God and meeting the needs of humanity.

- A third step recognizes the church exists for the purpose of making disciples and not for having meetings and conducting business. Yet, many in church life continue to view the church as the place for taking care of "religious business." The church is about so much more. It is meant to be a place where disciples are enlisted and nurtured.

- Healthy congregations will also possess a healthy balance. It is a serious error for a church to become heavily focused on any one area of church life. For example, being healthy requires a balanced diet. And to develop a healthy life as a member of the body of Christ will require a needed balance as well. Specifically, the following needs will be required in congregational life: evangelism; education; exaltation (worship); encouragement (fellowship); and equipping members to effectively serve.

In conclusion, having healthy churches will equate to having healthy Christians. And having healthy Christians will result in having healthy churches. To have healthy churches there is the need to have members who are helped to remain healthy. Please pay attention to the following table. It attempts to contrast a healthy member of the body of Christ with an unhealthy member.

Membership Health	
Health Is Present	**Health Is Absent**
When discipleship is stressed	When church membership is stressed
When ministry is practiced	When meetings are practiced
When God and others are in view	When self and church are in view
When biblical study is enjoyed and exercised	When biblical study is largely ignored
When weekly public worship is practiced	When weekly public worship is infrequent
When spirituality is pursued	When spirituality is not pursued
When positive attitudes are in evidence	When negative attitudes are in evidence
When prayer is daily practiced	When prayer is rarely practiced
When serving is present	When being served is present
When one regularly witnesses to others	When one rarely witnesses to others
When one anticipates the future and heaven	When one is insensitive to the future and heaven

Reflections

1. Do you think the analogy given by Carl Ketcherside in this chapter is a good one to use with regard to emphasizing the restoration of the church?

2. Can you explain the difference between what is essential and what is not essential in a church?

3. According to the author, why do congregations become sidetracked in non-essentials?

4. Would you conclude your congregation is engaged in seeking the lost? Or, is your congregation engaged in stealing members from other churches?

5. Why is transfer growth not a healthy way for a congregation to grow?

6. What kind of congregations serve as healthy models from which to learn?

7.   After reading this chapter would you conclude that preaching is an important and healthy congregational benchmark?

8.   Can you explain what the author means by connective sermons?

9.   List some of the aspects of an unhealthy church given by the author.

10. Instruction was given in this chapter for turning an unhealthy church around to become a healthy church. What counsel was given by the author?

11. What threat lies in front of our communities today when our congregations are unhealthy?

Conclusion

—⟋⟍—

Together the author and reader have been on a rather long and tedious journey in this volume. Hopefully, it has opened the eyes of the reader to some of the significant dangers and pitfalls confronting churches today. The focus throughout this book has been on having a magnificent church in these unhealthy times. It has not been an attempt to find fault with churches. Instead, it has been an effort to rescue congregations from their current ongoing battle with amnesia.

There is a major reason why believers need to work toward rescuing congregations from their amnesiac malaise in these dark times. Failure to do so shatters the hopes for having a healthy planet for ourselves and all those who will follow. Rather than making progress toward a healthy

Christian world persons face the possibility of seeing the culture become a pagan culture.

A major motion picture has recently been released. The title of the movie is, *The End of the Spear.* It is based on the true story of five American missionaries who went to South Africa with the gospel. Their names were Jim Eliot, Nate Saint, Roger Youderian, Pete Fleming and Ed McCully. Their chief aim was to bring the natives out of the darkness of sin and into the light of the glorious gospel. In the process these godly men lost their lives to savage pagans in this distant land.

Why the hostility and rejection of God's people? It was due to the nature of life in that remote, savage, and non-Christian land. The faithful witness of these five men, however, has resulted in a radical turnaround for several of these South Africans. There are now people in South Africa who know Christ and seek to serve Him. Without the Christian witness of these faithful martyrs there would have been no story of transformation and health to tell about today.

America has not been known as a land of paganism and without the gospel of Christ. Instead, it has been a land blessed with a large number of Christian witnesses, and has experienced the impact of the transforming gospel within its borders. It knows little of the type savagery toward Christianity prompting the ruthless killing of these faithful missionaries.

But when congregations are unhealthy, America faces the danger and threat of seeing a Christian land degenerate into a pagan land. For persons are always just one generation away from seeing Christianity extinguished and for paganism to reign. This is why the health of churches is a vital issue for these dark times. There can be no lasting growth for the church through having conversions, if the health of congregations is at risk.

Yet, the church can make a difference in society. It can avoid the serious spiritual toxins at work within it, and that seek to undermine it. Mac Brunson and Ergun Caner see other kinds of toxins operating within our churches when they "... gather to whine, complain, and fight."[24] It is time for the church to awaken to the harmful cancers threatening it, and to develop into a force of dedicated and disciplined disciples.

In the time of Hitler's ruthless rampage the church served as a light in the horrendous darkness surrounding it. That was the view of Albert Einstein. Listen to Einstein's words: "Only the church stood squarely across the path of Hitler's campaign for suppressing the truth. I never had any special interest in the church before, but now I feel a great affection and admiration for it because the church alone has had the courage and persistence to stand for intellectual and moral freedom. I am forced to confess that what I once despised I now praise unreservedly."[25]

The author also has a special affection and fondness for the church. In fact, he has always enjoyed this connection. He has been in the life of the church in both its good and bad times. And with all of its warts and wrinkles the church is still a great reservoir of light to those who are hungry and searching. It is the author's desire to see it be a healthy church for these unhealthy times. In short, he wants to see it become a magnificent church and not continue as a malignant church. Join the author in the ministry of seeing this does not happen in the present time.

Notes

—w—

1. Bill Esaum, *Dancing With Dinosaurs.* (Nashville: Abingdon, 1993).

2. Rick Warren, *The Purpose Driven Church.* (Grand Rapids: Zondervan, 1995), 27.

3. Paul Nixon, *Healing Spiritual Amnesia.* (Nashville: Abingdon, 2004).

4. Jim Collins, *Good To Great.* (New York City: Harper Business Essentials, 2001).

5. Warren Bennis and Burt Nanus, *Leaders.* (New York City: Harper Perennial, 1985).

6.   Tom Clegg and Warren Bird, *Lost in America.* (Loveland: Group, 2001), 35. The authors clearly state: "Churches are going out of business."

7.   Divisive issues are in existence in both the church at Rome, and at Corinth. A careful reading of each letter makes this clear.

8.   George Barna, *Revolution.* (Wheaton: Tyndale House, 2005).

9.   Reggie McNeal, *The Present Future.* The Jossey-Bass Leadership Series. (San Francisco: Jossey Bass, 2003), 11.

10.   William M. Easum, *Sacred Cows Make Gourmet Burgers.* (Nashville: Abingdon, 1995), 12.

11.   Ibid., 54-55.

12.   Ibid., 51.

13.   Ibid., 49-57.

14. George Barna, *The Frog in the Kettle.* (Ventura: Regal Books, 1990).

15. Note the instruction of Jesus in John 15:5; and the teaching of Paul in II Corinthians 3:5.

16. Gary McIntosh and Glen Martin, *Finding Them, Keeping Them.* (Nashville: Broadman, 1992).

17. Phil Vassar, *This Is God.* (Nashville: Rutledge Hill, 2003), 31.

18. Enos Dowling, *The Restoration Movement.* (Cincinnati: Standard, 1964).

19. W. F. Lown, *The Restoration Movement and its Meaning For Today.* The First Annual B.D. Phillips Memorial Lectureship. (Kimberlin Heights, TN: Johnson Bible College, 1970), 12-13.

20. William Chadwick, *Stealing Sheep.* (Downers Grove: InterVarsity, 2001).

21. Mark Galli and Craig Brian Larson, *Preaching that Connects*. (Grand Rapids: Zondervan, 1994).

Craig A. Loscalzo, *Preaching Sermons That Connect*. (Downers Grove: InterVarsity Press, 1992).

Alan Nelson, *Creating Messages that Connect*. (Loveland: Group, 2004).

22. Thom S. Rainer, *Surprising Insights From the Unchurched*. (Grand Rapids: Zondervan, 2001).

23. Michael Fabarez, *Preaching That Changes Lives*. (Nashville: Thomas Nelson Publishers, 2002), 5.

24. Mac Brunson and Ergun Caner, *Why Churches Die*. (Nashville: Broadman & Holman, 2005), 204.

25. Bob Kelly, *Worth Repeating*. (Grand Rapids: Kregel, 2003), 55.

About the Author

—៱៱—

B ill Campbell has served as minister, college and semi-
nary educator, writer, consultant, seminar instructor,
special speaker, mentor, and community leader. He holds
degrees from the following institutions: BA Degree from
St. Louis Christian College; MDiv Degree from Lincoln
Christian Seminary; DMin Degree from Eden Theological
Seminary; and a PhD Degree from American Christian
Seminary.

In 2001 **Dr. Campbell** received the Distinguished Alumni
Award from St. Louis Christian College. Later, in 2003 he
was elected to honorary membership in Delta Epsilon Chi
Honor Society. This award was in recognition of outstanding
intellectual achievement, approved Christian character, and
the effective exercise of leadership gifts in advancing the
cause of Christ. Congregational and academic services have

characterized Dr. Campbell's career. He has also served as President of the Rotary Club of Will Rogers; served on the school board of Jennings Public Schools; a member of the Flora Academic Foundation and Ethics Commission; and as President of both the Tulsa and Flora Ministerial Alliance.

Dr. Campbell is the father of five children and seven grandchildren. He and his wife Susan live in Flora, Illinois, where he serves as Senior Minister of First Christian Church. He has written a previous book entitled, *The Magnificent Journey.*

Available Services

—〰—

The author, Dr. Bill Campbell, is available for various
engagements.

His services include:

consulting with congregations and ministers;

leading seminars; and

other public speaking occasions.

Dr. Campbell may be contacted as follows:

Email: fccbrc@hotmail.com

Printed in the United States
62472LVS00001B/1-141

9 781600 347139